PENGUIN

OF MICE AND MEN AND
THE MOON IS DOWN

Born in Salinas, California, in 1902, JOHN STEINBECK grew up in a fertile agriculture valley about twenty-five miles from the Pacific Coast—and both valley and coast would serve as settings for some of his best fiction. In 1919 he went to Stanford University, where he intermittently enrolled in literature and writing courses until he left in 1925 without taking a degree. During the next five years he supported himself as a laborer and journalist in New York City and then as a caretaker for a Lake Tahoe estate, all the time working on his first novel, *Cup of Gold* (1929). After marriage and a move to Pacific Grove, he published two California fictions, *The Pastures of Heaven* (1932) and *To a God Unknown* (1933), and worked on short stories later collected in *The Long Valley* (1938). Popular success and financial security came only with *Tortilla Flat* (1935), stories about Monterey's paisanos. A ceaseless experimenter throughout his career, Steinbeck changed courses regularly. Three powerful novels of the late 1930s focused on the California laboring class: *In Dubious Battle* (1936), *Of Mice and Men* (1937), and the book considered by many his finest, *The Grapes of Wrath* (1939). Early in the 1940s, Steinbeck became a filmmaker with *The Forgotten Village* (1941) and a serious student of marine biology with *Sea of Cortez* (1941). He devoted his services to the war, writing *Bombs Away* (1942) and the controversial play-novelette *The Moon Is Down* (1942). *Cannery Row* (1945), *The Wayward Bus* (1947), *The Pearl* (1947), *A Russian Journal* (1948), another experimental drama, *Burning Bright* (1950), and *The Log from the* Sea of Cortez (1951) preceded publication of the monumental *East of Eden* (1952), an ambitious saga of the Salinas Valley and his own family's history. The last decades of his life were spent in New York City and Sag Harbor with his third wife, with whom he traveled widely. Later books included *Sweet Thursday* (1954), *The Short Reign of Pippin IV: A Fabrication* (1957), *Once There Was a War* (1958), *The Winter of Our Discontent*

(1961), *Travels with Charley in Search of America* (1962), *America and Americans* (1966), and the posthumously published *Journal of a Novel: The* East of Eden *Letters* (1969), *Viva Zapata!* (1975), *The Acts of King Arthur and His Noble Knights* (1976), and *Working Days: The Journals of* The Grapes of Wrath (1989). He died in 1968, having won a Nobel Prize in 1962.

JAMES EARL JONES was born in Mississippi, raised in Michigan, and moved to New York City after graduating from the University of Michigan and serving in the military. Supporting himself by working as a janitor, he struggled to make it as an actor and made his Broadway debut in 1957. Based on his success in the theater, he began to be cast in small television roles. In the 1960s Jones was one of the first African American actors to appear regularly in daytime soap operas, and he made his film debut in 1964 in Stanley Kubrick's *Dr. Strangelove*. In 1969 Jones won a Tony Award for his breakthrough role as boxer Jack Johnson in the Broadway hit *The Great White Hope* (which also garnered him an Oscar nomination for the 1970 film adaptation). In addition to his distinguished career on stage and screen, Jones is an iconic vocal presence in films such as the Star Wars trilogy and *The Lion King*. Jones is the recipient of many awards as an actor—two Tonys, four Emmys, a Golden Globe, two Cable ACEs, two OBIEs, five Drama Desks, and a Grammy—and has been honored with the National Medal of Arts in 1992 and the John F. Kennedy Center Honor in December 2002. In January 2009, the Screen Actors Guild bestowed Jones with a Lifetime Achievement Award.

JOHN STEINBECK

Of Mice and Men

A PLAY IN THREE ACTS

and

The Moon Is Down

A PLAY IN TWO PARTS

With a Foreword by JAMES EARL JONES

PENGUIN BOOKS

PENGUIN BOOKS

Published by the Penguin Group
Penguin Group (USA) Inc., 375 Hudson Street, New York, New York 10014, U.S.A.
Penguin Group (Canada), 90 Eglinton Avenue East, Suite 700, Toronto,
Ontario, Canada M4P 2Y3 (a division of Pearson Penguin Canada Inc.)
Penguin Books Ltd, 80 Strand, London WC2R 0RL, England
Penguin Ireland, 25 St Stephen's Green, Dublin 2, Ireland (a division of Penguin Books Ltd)
Penguin Group (Australia), 250 Camberwell Road, Camberwell,
Victoria 3124, Australia (a division of Pearson Australia Group Pty Ltd)
Penguin Books India Pvt Ltd, 11 Community Centre, Panchsheel Park, New Delhi–110 017, India
Penguin Group (NZ), 67 Apollo Drive, Rosedale, North Shore 0632,
New Zealand (a division of Pearson New Zealand Ltd)
Penguin Books (South Africa) (Pty) Ltd, 24 Sturdee Avenue,
Rosebank, Johannesburg 2196, South Africa

Penguin Books Ltd, Registered Offices: 80 Strand, London WC2R 0RL, England

Of Mice and Men: A Play in Three Acts
First published in the United States of America by Covici-Friede 1937
Published by The Viking Press 1938
Published in Penguin Books 2009

The Moon Is Down: Play in Two Parts
First published in the United States of America by The Viking Press 1942
Published in Penguin Books 2009

This volume with a foreword by James Earl Jones published in Penguin Books 2010

1 3 5 7 9 10 8 6 4 2

Of Mice and Men: A Play in Three Acts
Copyright John Steinbeck, 1937
Copyright renewed John Steinbeck, 1965
All rights reserved

The Moon Is Down: Play in Two Parts
Copyright John Steinbeck, 1942
Copyright renewed Elaine A. Steinbeck, Thom Steinbeck, and John Steinbeck IV, 1970
All rights reserved

Foreword copyright © James Earl Jones, 2010
All rights reserved

ISBN 978-0-14-310613-5
CIP data available

Printed in the United States of America
Set in Sabon

Contents

Foreword

The best-laid schemes o' mice an' men Gang aft agley,
An' lea'e us nought but grief an' pain, For promis'd
joy!

—ROBERT BURNS, "TO A MOUSE," NOVEMBER 1785

Whether as a novelist or as a playwright, John Steinbeck is a favorite writer of actors. For workshop purposes, actors can just as easily parse dialogue from his novels as from his plays. In fact, Steinbeck said *Of Mice and Men* is "neither a novel nor a play but it is a kind of playable novel." In this very "playable novel," he uses dialogue to reveal time, place, character, and feeling—and that dialogue tends to be organic, not just exposition. It provides the exchange of ideas between characters as they reveal themselves to each other and to the reader or the audience.

Of Mice and Men is one of the best examples of Steinbeck's novels or plays to achieve this kind of revelation. The best-laid plans of mice and men often go awry, as it's commonly said. The desire of George and Lennie, the two migrant farm workers, to have a farm of their own is in no way a "best-laid plan." It is instead a vague dream—one of those perpetual daydreams that can lurk in the minds of people who suffer, and who have nothing to rely on but the company of their fellow creatures. Of the two men, Lennie has the least ability to fathom ideas. He depends upon the vision of the farm as his security blanket, and it is George who feeds this vision to him, always in private. George weaves the fantasy of this farm with the words of a story-teller. The words about the farm are Lennie's favorite words in life, even though he cannot remember any of them. George explains Lennie's mental state to strangers: "He got kicked in the head by a horse when he was a kid."

My first experience performing *Of Mice and Men* came in 1955 when several of us American Theatre Wing students were cast in an experimental production at the Walt Whitman Theatre at Brooklyn College. I took the role of Crooks, the black stable hand who has a broken and crooked back from being kicked by a horse. When my father, Robert Earl Jones, came to Brooklyn to see the production, he gave me the best praise a father could give his son in this business: "You can act." He didn't have to say more—that I was good or great. I knew that I was engaged with the words of this character, and I had begun to understand what that meant for an actor.

The real reward was to discover, under the direction of Yabo Yablonsky, the electric charge of getting in touch with the visceral feelings of Steinbeck's well-written characters. I found that when Crooks met Lennie, he felt an overwhelming delight that he had finally come across someone who was worse off than he was. The thrill of those cynical feelings carried me through the whole production.

My second chance to play *Of Mice and Men* would place me onstage as Lennie, with my father playing Crooks, at Purdue University's professional repertory theater in 1967, under the direction of Joe Stockdale. I had briefly met Steinbeck by that time, so I got in touch with him about the idea of a black actor playing a character he had conceived, I assumed, as a white character. Steinbeck said that I was probably worried about the scenes where the word "nigger" was voiced in Lennie's presence. He said Lennie would have no awareness of the construct of race. He would indeed understand meanness or hostility, but nothing embedded in social code. According to Steinbeck, Lennie wouldn't even know what the word meant. It would simply breeze through one ear and out the other.

There was a professor of psychology at the university who was a fan of the theater. When he saw a production of *A Streetcar Named Desire*, he thought that the actress playing Blanche actually possessed all of the signs of schizophrenia during her performance, although he admitted that his observations were only cursory and that she certainly was a good actress.

When he saw our production of *Of Mice and Men*, he decided to test me to see how close to Lennie's state I could come as an actor. He told me that when I played Lennie, he thought I had a temporary IQ of about seventy. He had me dress up as Lennie and come into his graduate studies laboratory to be tested—as Lennie, not as myself—by a student who was not aware of the production nor of who I was. I was able to do my version of Lennie in response to the IQ phases of the test, but when it came to the Rorschach phase, I could respond only as myself. At one point the student quietly left the room and went to the section where the professor and the rest of his class were observing through a one-way mirror and said, "There is something screwy happening in there. You should have him committed right away before he does something violent. He's obviously dangerous." His comment about "Lennie" was prophetic.

In my third encounter with *Of Mice and Men*, I played Lennie again, this time in 1974 at Southern Methodist University at the Bob Hope Theatre, under the direction of Edwin Sherin. Because we were in a university setting, the staff was able to give me and Kevin Conway (who was playing George) an opportunity to visit a local "home for retardates," as such institutions were called at that time. While at the home, we were advised to be aware of how the patients there lived on a different plane from so-called normal people, and about the caution we needed to exercise in any exchange of emotion with the patients. For example, any gesture that could be interpreted as affection could easily be magnified in the perception of the patient, who might be closed off mentally but whose senses were wide open, without social inhibitions.

I went there with the conviction that when Lennie says to George, "If you don't want me, I can go right in them hills, and find a cave," Lennie meant just exactly that, and he was capable of doing that. However, I came away convinced that Lennie could in no way go off and live in a cave. With that knowledge came a sad realization about the character of George: he carried all the social responsibility for this other human being, and he knew that since there was no way that Lennie would ever find his way to an institution that could care for him, he would more likely end up in prison, where he would certainly die.

We returned to the rehearsals at SMU, and on through the Broadway run of that production, with the realization that George was a truly tragic hero because he knew from the first moment he entered the stage that he would someday have to kill Lennie—and that only he could or should commit that sacrifice.

I don't know whether Steinbeck had that in mind or not.

He had told a reporter in 1937 that Lennie was a real person—a man he had worked alongside on a ranch in the 1920s. Steinbeck was a witness when the real Lennie killed a ranch foreman with a pitchfork because the foreman had fired Lennie's friend. "We couldn't stop him until it was too late," Steinbeck remembered. Lennie was then incarcerated in an "insane asylum" in California.

British director Tyrone Guthrie, founder of the Guthrie Theater in Minneapolis, once said that every play is only the tip of the iceberg of a mass of humanity, and that the submerged part often contains elements the author has chosen not to write, or is not even aware of himself—but different productions, actors, and directors may keep on discovering new depths as long as the play survives. Whatever Steinbeck's intention, my experience with the depths of this play has led me to see George as a classical heroic character and Lennie as the "elemental God of pathos."

Other characters in the drama are examples of people with nothing in life but the company of their fellow creatures.

The cook has a dog who is old and blind and starting to stink. Everyone else in the bunkhouse wants to get rid of that dog, but he is the cook's last deep connection to a fellow creature. The cook is eventually worn down and he allows one of the men to take the dog out and shoot him, an act that foreshadows Lennie's fate.

The girl—Curley's wife—who is to become the inadvertent cause of Lennie's troubles, has made the mistake of marrying the boss's son when what she really wanted was to go to Hollywood and become a movie star. She finds her life devoid of the comfort of fellow creatures, and that loneliness drives her out to the barn where Lennie is hiding a puppy he's just destroyed by petting it too passionately.

In this scene, Steinbeck writes a dialogue between two people who have no idea what the other is talking about. She is talking about her Hollywood dreams, and he, the fragments of the fantasy-farm that George has spun in his mind. When that verbal communication breaks down, there is nothing left but touch.

I had an acting coach once who said that I might picture Lennie as not being able to think—but the sad truth is that Lennie thinks too much, but of only one thing, and that is the softness of the fur of rabbits. My coach said Lennie has a Ph.D. in the softness of the fur of rabbits. Too often Lennie is played for his humor, and as being a big cuddly bear, but Lennie is a killer, a very dangerous creature. Curley's wife discovers this reality too late after she allows Lennie to stroke her hair. Finally, George shoots Lennie to save him from the lynch mob that is pursuing him.

"Try to understand each other," Steinbeck wrote in his journal in the late 1930s. "You can't hate men if you know them." When he received the Nobel Prize in Literature in 1962, the Swedish Academy honored Steinbeck in part because "His sympathies always go out to the oppressed, to the misfits and the distressed. . . ." We can discover and rediscover this in George and Lennie and the other characters in Steinbeck's powerful "playable novel."

> BANQUO: *How goes the night, boy?*
> FLEANCE: *The moon is down; I have not heard the clock.*
>
> —*Macbeth*, Act II, Scene I

I have not had experience as an actor or audience member with *The Moon Is Down*, but after studying it, I've come to appreciate how John Steinbeck's emphasis on dialogue and language enfolds me in the life of the characters.

In the novel and the play, *The Moon Is Down* is another of Steinbeck's dramas that reveals time, place, character, and feeling through compelling dialogue. The play qualifies as propaganda, but that does not necessarily disqualify it as valid literature. At the beginning of World War II, from the invasion of Poland on, Steinbeck was one of many writers who used their talents to address events that threatened to change the world. Such writers as Steinbeck and Lillian Hellman, for instance, helped to focus attention on the dangers of the invasion of one country by another, more aggressive country whose ultimate aim was global conquest.

The Moon Is Down, published in 1942, came a year after Hellman's play *Watch on the Rhine*, which appeared in

1941 and won the New York Drama Critics' Circle Award. (There was a film version of her play in 1943.) In *Watch on the Rhine*, the setting is not an international battleground but an upper-class Washington, D.C., suburban home where two adversarial refugees meet. One is the anti-Nazi son-in-law of the lady of the house, a German national, fresh from fighting fascists in the Spanish Civil War. The other is the aristocratic and opportunistic husband of a houseguest. He is a Romanian national but his sentiments, if not pro-Nazi, are certainly corrupt enough to place him on the side of the "bad guys." Hellman's genius lay in weaving revealing conversations between highly "civilized" people to expose their baseness or their nobility. She never let melodrama embarrass her. She invested her characters with her own outspoken political passion. She was a playwright/activist who pulled no punches and certainly would have worn the word "propaganda" proudly. She felt an urgent need to set up a "watch on the Potomac."

In contrast, Steinbeck keeps it very simple in *The Moon Is Down* by not even identifying the nationalities of his characters. But with a few strokes suggestive of weaponry, uniforms, and tactics, it is quite obvious that he is talking about the Nazi invasion of some other, more vulnerable country. He does not rely on specific labels because he wants the audience to think only of the invaders and the occupied people—to see them in universal terms, as human beings in conflict. His approach renders his work more timeless.

Another way to contrast Steinbeck's kind of propaganda play to the work of others is to consider *Red Dawn*, a motion picture written and directed by John Milius. Released in 1984, *Red Dawn* is an updated, transposed story based on *The Moon Is Down*. The movie stars Patrick Swayze and Charlie Sheen and depicts the occupation of the western United States by a coalition of Cuban and Soviet forces. John Milius highlights a strong theme exploited by

John Steinbeck—the confiscation of civilian firearms by invading forces. Having worked with John Milius on *Conan the Barbarian*, I know him to be staunch on Second Amendment rights, so that was a natural choice for him.

Steinbeck expresses considerable advocacy through two of his "good guy" characters, who are seeking assistance and weapons from allies:

> WILL ANDERS to MAYOR ORDEN: *I've heard that in England there are still men who do not dare put weapons in the hands of common people.*
> MAYOR ORDEN to WILL ANDERS: . . . *If such people still govern England and America, the world is lost. . . .*

Probably to the dismay of John Milius, world events have been more fluid than might have been expected. The Soviet Union has ended, and U.S. and Cuban relationships seem to be softening, so the propaganda value of *Red Dawn* is diminished and less relevant, partly because the story was quite simplistic. Since it is a film in which dialogue sometimes takes second place to action, there is less opportunity for the film to explore human nature on both sides through language and dialogue. The Soviet-Cuban coalition characters are simplified bad guys, and the occupied Americans are highly sentimentalized good guys. The movie's main value comes in its action sequences that, according to my son, are quite impressive. He watched the film with me and liked it very much, being a member of the "action" generation.

In the film, Ron O'Neal, the African American actor first made famous by his performance as the drug dealer in *Super Fly*, plays the highest-ranking Cuban officer. Up to his final scene in the movie, Milius directs him in pure Cold War anti-Castro bad guy terms, with very little depth to illuminate him. One theme that Milius does bring out in the

Swayze-Sheen "good guy" contingent is the loss of innocence: "Don't cry, don't ever cry again."

Oversimplified dialogue between characters tends to shut
the audience out of a story, as in the movie, whereas com-
plex dialogue between people who respect each other, at
least as human beings, tends to draw the audience in, as in
Steinbeck's play.

Steinbeck provides this rich complexity in *The Moon Is
Down*. The occupied people gradually lose their innocence
and vulnerability, leaving them more ruthless and determined to resist the invaders. In general, Steinbeck wants us,
as the audience, to think not of particulars, but only of the
eternal invader and the eternal occupied people. I believe he
was trying to avoid the kind of simplistic propaganda that
strips situations and characters of dimension, and to move
beyond propaganda into universal truth. He wanted us to
look at all of the people involved as human beings, not as
Nazis or Allies. He wanted to take us as deep as he could
into the souls of the characters—not for sympathy's sake
but for understanding.

Steinbeck even uses touches of humor to add dimension
to the play as he exposes the folly on both sides. The town
mayor, a "good guy," is also, at first, a bit of a henpecked
priss. The lower-ranked soldiers of the invading force are
an array of clowns, no two alike, yet they are not
stereotypes—more specimens. But it is Colonel Lanser, the
highest in command of the invaders, who has about him the
professional and intellectual ruthlessness of a man caught
up in what he knows to be insanity.

Having invested the colonel with that sharpness of mind,
Steinbeck uses it in the exchanges of dialogue to reveal the
character of Lanser as well as the occupied people he is
talking to. Through their jokes, his own soldiers inadver-
tently allow themselves an awareness of the insanity. One
soldier speaks of a rumor that the leader (Hitler) is crazy—a

fact that has not escaped notice nor does it surprise anyone outside of the invading regime's realm. But the idea triggers a sense of absurdism in the ranks of the invading force.

The longer the invasion lasts, the more the friction caused by the occupation begins to wear down both sides. The soldiers came with certitude and hubris, expecting cheers and flowers; they came from hometowns where coffee shops offered them cakes served by pretty girls who smiled at them. Now they only see girls who do not smile except to lure them into traps to assassinate them.

At this point of disillusionment, Colonel Lanser gives his men his redefinition of a soldier:

> You're not a man any more. You're a soldier. Your comfort is of no importance and your life not very much. . . . You must take orders and carry them out. Most of them will be unpleasant. But that's not your business. . . . They should have trained you for this. Not for cheers and flowers.

Gradually, the invader loses his crust of invincibility and his vulnerability is exposed. Likewise, as the occupied loses his innocence and vulnerability, he becomes the insurgent.

Steinbeck reveals all of this not through obvious propaganda or melodrama, but through gripping dialogue between two opposing forces of desperate men.

Steinbeck's fundamental goal was communication and understanding. He said, "I think that writing may be simply a method or technique for communication with other individuals; and its stimulus, the loneliness we are born to. In writing, perhaps we hope to achieve companionship."

In *Of Mice and Men*, *The Moon Is Down*, and another of his works, *Burning Bright*, Steinbeck experimented with a form he named the "play-novelette." In 1938, he wrote about what he hoped to achieve in this unique blend of fiction and drama: "In the reading of a novel there are involved only the author, the novel, and the reader," he said, "but in the seeing of a play there are the author, the play, the players, and the whole audience, and each one of these contributes a vital part to the whole effect."

Steinbeck's use of dialogue provides the connective tissue for the author, the actors, and the audience as they share the experience of his "play-novelettes." He said he hoped that through this experiment, the novel would "benefit by the discipline, the terseness of the drama," and the drama, in turn, "might achieve increased openness, freedom and versatility." He was afraid his experiment had failed—but for me and countless others, it has worked powerfully on the page and on the stage.

In his Nobel Prize acceptance speech in 1962, Steinbeck reflected on the necessity of meaningful dialogue and the power of the word: "Man himself has become our greatest hazard and our only hope. So that today, Saint John the Apostle may well be paraphrased: In the end is the *word*, and the word is *man*, and the word is *with* man."

JAMES EARL JONES

Source: John Steinbeck, "The Play-Novelette," in *America and Americans, and Selected Nonfiction*, edited by Susan Shillinglaw and Jackson J. Benson (New York: Viking, 2002), pp.155–57.

OF MICE AND MEN

A PLAY IN THREE ACTS

PERSONS IN THE PLAY

GEORGE   *A small, sharp-faced ranch hand*

LENNIE   *His huge, but not bright, companion*

SLIM   *A jerk-line skinner, a master workman*

CANDY   *An old swamper*

THE BOSS   *Superintendent of the ranch*

CURLEY   *The boss's son*

CURLEY'S WIFE

CARLSON   *A ranch hand*

WHIT   *A ranch hand*

CROOKS   *A negro stable buck*

CAST OF CHARACTERS

This play was first presented by Sam H. Harris at the Music Box Theatre on the evening of November 23, 1937, with the following cast:

GEORGE	*Wallace Ford*
LENNIE	*Broderick Crawford*
CANDY	*John F. Hamilton*
THE BOSS	*Thomas Findlay*
CURLEY	*Sam Byrd*
CURLEY'S WIFE	*Claire Luce*
SLIM	*Will Geer*
CARLSON	*Charles Slattery*
WHIT	*Walter Baldwin*
CROOKS	*Leigh Whipper*

Staged by George S. Kaufman
Settings by Donald Oenslager

SYNOPSIS OF SCENES

ACT ONE

SCENE I: A sandy bank of the Salinas River.
Thursday night.

SCENE II: The interior of a bunkhouse. Late
Friday morning.

ACT TWO

SCENE I: The same as Act I, Scene II.
About seven-thirty Friday evening.

SCENE II: The room of the stable buck, a lean-to.
Ten o'clock Saturday evening.

ACT THREE

SCENE I: One end of a great barn.
Mid-afternoon, Sunday.

SCENE II: Same as Act I, Scene I. Sunday night.

TIME: The present.

PLACE: An agricultural valley in Northern California.

ACT ONE

ACT ONE: SCENE I

Thursday night.
A sandy bank of the Salinas River sheltered with willows—one giant sycamore right, upstage.
The stage is covered with dry leaves. The feeling of the stage is sheltered and quiet.
Stage is lit by a setting sun.
Curtain rises on an empty stage. A sparrow is singing. There is a distant sound of ranch dogs barking aimlessly and one clear quail call. The quail call turns to a warning call and there is a beat of the flock's wings. Two figures are seen entering the stage in single file, with GEORGE, *the short man, coming in ahead of* LENNIE. *Both men are carrying blanket rolls. They approach the water. The small man throws down his blanket roll, the large man follows and then falls down and drinks from the river, snorting as he drinks.*

GEORGE [*irritably*]: Lennie, for God's sake, don't drink so much. [*Leans over and shakes* LENNIE.] Lennie, you hear me! You gonna be sick like you was last night.
LENNIE [*dips his whole head under, hat and all. As he sits upon the bank, his hat drips down the back*]: That's good. You drink some, George. You drink some too.
GEORGE [*kneeling and dipping his finger in the water*]: I ain't sure it's good water. Looks kinda scummy to me.

LENNIE [*imitates, dipping his finger also*]: Look at them wrinkles in the water, George. Look what I done.

GEORGE [*drinking from his cupped palm*]: Tastes all right. Don't seem to be runnin' much, though. Lennie, you oughtn' to drink water when it ain't running. [*Hopelessly.*] You'd drink water out of a gutter if you was thirsty. [*He throws a scoop of water into his face and rubs it around with his hand, pushes himself back and embraces his knees.* LENNIE, *after watching him, imitates him in every detail.*]

GEORGE [*beginning tiredly and growing angry as he speaks*]: God damn it, we could just as well of rode clear to the ranch. That bus driver didn't know what he was talkin' about. "Just a little stretch down the highway," he says. "Just a little stretch"—damn near four miles. I bet he didn't want to stop at the ranch gate. . . . I bet he's too damn lazy to pull up. Wonder he ain't too lazy to stop at Soledad at all! [*Mumbling.*] Just a little stretch down the road.

LENNIE [*timidly*]: George?

GEORGE: Yeh . . . what you want?

LENNIE: Where we goin', George?

GEORGE [*jerks down his hat furiously*]: So you forgot that already, did you? So I got to tell you again! Jeez, you're a crazy bastard!

LENNIE [*softly*]: I forgot. I tried not to forget, honest to God, I did!

GEORGE: Okay, okay, I'll tell you again. . . . [*With sarcasm.*] I ain't got nothin' to do. Might just as well spen' all my time tellin' you things. You forgit 'em and I tell you again.

LENNIE [*continuing on from his last speech*]: I tried and tried, but it didn't do no good. I remember about the rabbits, George!

GEORGE: The hell with the rabbits! You can't remember

nothing but them rabbits. You remember settin' in that gutter on Howard Street and watchin' that blackboard?

LENNIE [*delightedly*]: Oh, sure! I remember that . . . but . . . wha'd we do then? I remember some girls come by, and you says—

GEORGE: The hell with what I says! You remember about us goin' in Murray and Ready's and they give us work cards and bus tickets?

LENNIE: [*confidently*]: Oh, sure, George . . . I remember that now. [*Puts his hand into his side coat-pocket; his confidence vanishes. Very gently.*] . . . George?

GEORGE: Huh?

LENNIE [*staring at the ground in despair*]: I ain't got mine. I musta lost it.

GEORGE: You never had none. I got both of 'em here. Think I'd let you carry your own work card?

LENNIE [*with tremendous relief*]: I thought I put it in my side pocket. [*Puts his hand in his pocket again.*]

GEORGE [*looking sharply at him; and as he looks,* LENNIE *brings his hand out of his pocket*]: Wha'd you take out of that pocket?

LENNIE [*cleverly*]: Ain't a thing in my pocket.

GEORGE: I know there ain't. You got it in your hand now. What you got in your hand?

LENNIE: I ain't got nothing, George! Honest!

GEORGE: Come on, give it here!

LENNIE [*holds his closed hand away from* GEORGE]: It's on'y a mouse!

GEORGE: A mouse? A live mouse?

LENNIE: No . . . just a dead mouse. [*Worriedly.*] I didn't kill it. Honest. I found it. I found it dead.

GEORGE: Give it here!

LENNIE: Leave me have it, George.

GEORGE [*sternly*]: Give it here! [LENNIE *reluctantly gives him the mouse.*] What do you want of a dead mouse, anyway?

LENNIE [*in a propositional tone*]: I was petting it with my thumb while we walked along.

GEORGE: Well, you ain't pettin' no mice while you walk with me. Now let's see if you can remember where we're going. [GEORGE *throws it across the water into the brush.*]

LENNIE [*looks startled and then in embarrassment hides his face against his knees*]: I forgot again.

GEORGE: Jesus Christ! [*Resignedly.*] Well, look, we are gonna work on a ranch like the one we come from up north.

LENNIE: Up north?

GEORGE: In Weed!

LENNIE: Oh, sure I remember—in Weed.

GEORGE [*still with exaggerated patience*]: That ranch we're goin' to is right down there about a quarter mile. We're gonna go in and see the boss.

LENNIE [*repeats as a lesson*]: And see the boss!

GEORGE: Now, look! I'll give him the work tickets, but you ain't gonna say a word. You're just gonna stand there and not say nothing.

LENNIE: Not say nothing!

GEORGE: If he finds out what a crazy bastard you are, we won't get no job. But if he sees you work before he hears you talk, we're set. You got that?

LENNIE: Sure, George . . . sure. I got that.

GEORGE: Okay. Now when we go in to see the boss, what you gonna do?

LENNIE [*concentrating*]: I . . . I . . . I ain't gonna say nothing . . . jus' gonna stand there.

GEORGE [*greatly relieved*]: Good boy, that's swell! Now say that over two or three times so you sure won't forget it.

LENNIE [*drones softly under his breath*]: I ain't gonna say nothing . . . I ain't gonna say nothing. . . . [*Trails off into a whisper.*]

GEORGE: And you ain't gonna do no bad things like you done in Weed neither.

LENNIE [*puzzled*]: Like I done in Weed?

GEORGE: So you forgot that too, did you?

LENNIE [*triumphantly*]: They run us out of Weed!

GEORGE [*disgusted*]: Run us out, hell! We run! They was lookin' for us, but they didn't catch us.

LENNIE [*happily*]: I didn't forget that, you bet.

GEORGE [*lies back on the sand, crosses his hands under his head. And again* LENNIE *imitates him*]: God, you're a lot of trouble! I could get along so easy and nice, if I didn't have you on my tail. I could live so easy!

LENNIE [*hopefully*]: We gonna work on a ranch, George.

GEORGE: All right, you got that. But we're gonna sleep here tonight, because . . . I want to. I want to sleep out. [*The light is going fast, dropping into evening. A little wind whirls into the clearing and blows leaves. A dog howls in the distance.*]

LENNIE: Why ain't we goin' on to the ranch to get some supper? They got supper at the ranch.

GEORGE: No reason at all. I just like it here. Tomorrow we'll be goin' to work. I seen thrashing machines on the way down; that means we'll be buckin' grain bags. Bustin' a gut liftin' up them bags. Tonight I'm gonna lay right here an' look up! Tonight there ain't a grain bag or a boss in the world. Tonight, the drinks is on the . . . house. Nice house we got here, Lennie.

LENNIE [*gets up on his knees and looks down at* GEORGE, *plaintively*]: Ain't we gonna have no supper?

GEORGE: Sure we are. You gather up some dead willow sticks. I got three cans of beans in my bindle. I'll open 'em up while you get a fire ready. We'll eat 'em cold.

LENNIE [*companionably*]: I like beans with ketchup.

GEORGE: Well, we ain't got no ketchup. You go get wood, and don't you fool around none. Be dark before long. [LENNIE *lumbers to his feet and disappears into the brush.* GEORGE *gets out the bean cans, opens two of them, suddenly turns his head and listens. A little sound of splashing comes from the direction that* LENNIE *has taken.* GEORGE *looks after him; shakes his head.* LENNIE *comes back carrying a few small willow sticks in his hand.*] All right, give me that mouse.

LENNIE [*with elaborate pantomime of innocence*]: What, George? I ain't got no mouse.

GEORGE [*holding out his hand*]: Come on! Give it to me! You ain't puttin' nothing over. [LENNIE *hesitates, backs away, turns and looks as if he were going to run. Coldly.*] You gonna give me that mouse or do I have to take a sock at you?

LENNIE: Give you what, George?

GEORGE: You know goddamn well, what! I want that mouse!

LENNIE [*almost in tears*]: I don't know why I can't keep it. It ain't nobody's mouse. I didn' steal it! I found it layin' right beside the road. [GEORGE *snaps his fingers sharply, and* LENNIE *lays the mouse in his hand.*] I wasn't doin' nothing bad with it. Just stroking it. That ain't bad.

GEORGE [*stands up and throws the mouse as far as he can into the brush, then he steps to the pool, and washes his hands*]: You crazy fool! Thought you could get away with it, didn't you? Don't you think I could see your feet was wet where you went in the water to get it? [LENNIE *whimpers like a puppy.*] Blubbering like a baby. Jesus Christ, a big guy like you! [LENNIE *tries to control himself, but his lips quiver and his face works with an effort.* GEORGE *puts his hand on* LENNIE'S *shoulder for a moment.*] Aw, Lennie, I ain't takin' it away just for meanness. That mouse ain't fresh. Besides, you broke it pettin' it. You get a mouse that's fresh and I'll let you keep it a little while.

LENNIE: I don't know where there is no other mouse. I remember a lady used to give 'em to me. Ever' one she got she used to give it to me, but that lady ain't here no more.

GEORGE: Lady, huh! . . . Give me them sticks there. . . . Don't even remember who that lady was. That was your own Aunt Clara. She stopped givin' 'em to you. You always killed 'em.

LENNIE [*sadly and apologetically*]: They was so little. I'd pet 'em and pretty soon they bit my fingers and then I pinched their head a little bit and then they was dead . . . because they was so little. I wish we'd get the rabbits pretty soon, George. They ain't so little.

GEORGE: The hell with the rabbits! Come on, let's eat! [*The light has continued to go out of the scene so that when* GEORGE *lights the fire, it is the major light on the stage.* GEORGE *hands one of the open cans of beans to* LEN-NIE.] There's enough beans for four men.

LENNIE [*sitting on the other side of the fire, speaks patiently*]: I like 'em with ketchup.

GEORGE [*explodes*]: Well, we ain't got any. Whatever we ain't got, that's what you want. God Almighty, if I was alone, I could live so easy. I could go get a job of work and no trouble. No mess . . . and when the end of the month come, I could take my fifty bucks and go into town and get whatever I want. Why, I could stay in a cat-house all night. I could eat any place I want. Order any damn thing.

LENNIE [*plaintively, but softly*]: I didn't want no ketchup.

GEORGE [*continuing violently*]: I could do that every damn month. Get a gallon of whiskey or set in a pool room and play cards or shoot pool. [LENNIE *gets up to his knees and looks over the fire, with frightened face*.] And what have I got? [*Disgustedly.*] I got *you*. You can't keep a job and you lose me every job I get!

LENNIE [*in terror*]: I don't mean nothing, George.

GEORGE: Just keep me shovin' all over the country all the time. And that ain't the worst—you get in trouble. You do bad things and I got to get you out. It ain't bad people that raises hell. It's dumb ones. [*He shouts.*] You crazy son-of-a-bitch, you keep me in hot water all the time. [LENNIE *is trying to stop* GEORGE'S *flow of words with his hands. Sarcastically.*] You just wanta feel that girl's dress. Just wanta pet it like it was a mouse. Well, how the hell'd she know you just wanta feel her dress? How'd she know you'd just hold onto it like it was a mouse?

LENNIE [*in a panic*]: I didn't mean to, George!

GEORGE: Sure you didn't mean to. You didn't mean for her to yell bloody hell, either. You didn't mean for us to hide in the irrigation ditch all day with guys out lookin' for us with guns. Alla time it's something you didn't mean. God damn it, I wish I could put you in a cage with a million mice and let them pet *you*. [GEORGE'S *anger leaves him suddenly. For the first time he seems to see the expression of terror on* LENNIE'S *face. He looks down ashamedly at the fire, and maneuvers some beans onto the blade of his pocket-knife and puts them into his mouth.*]

LENNIE [*after a pause*]: George! [GEORGE *purposely does not answer him.*] George?

GEORGE: What do you want?

LENNIE: I was only foolin', George. I don't want no ketchup. I wouldn't eat no ketchup if it was right here beside me.

GEORGE [*with a sullenness of shame*]: If they was some here you could have it. And if I had a thousand bucks I'd buy ya a bunch of flowers.

LENNIE: I wouldn't eat no ketchup, George. I'd leave it all for you. You could cover your beans so deep with it, and I wouldn't touch none of it.

GEORGE [*refusing to give in from his sullenness, refusing to look at* LENNIE]: When I think of the swell time I could have without you, I go nuts. I never git no peace!

LENNIE: You want I should go away and leave you alone?

GEORGE: Where the hell could you go?

LENNIE: Well, I could . . . I could go off in the hills there. Some place I could find a cave.

GEORGE: Yeah, how'd ya eat? You ain't got sense enough to find nothing to eat.

LENNIE: I'd find things. I don't need no nice food with ketchup. I'd lay out in the sun and nobody would hurt me. And if I found a mouse—why, I could keep it. Wouldn't nobody take it away from me.

GEORGE [*at last he looks up*]: I been mean, ain't I?

LENNIE [*presses his triumph*]: If you don't want me, I can go right in them hills, and find a cave. I can go away any time.

GEORGE: No. Look! I was just foolin' ya. 'Course I want you to stay with me. Trouble with mice is you always kill 'em. [*He pauses.*] Tell you what I'll do, Lennie. First chance I get I'll find you a pup. Maybe you wouldn't kill it. That would be better than mice. You could pet it harder.

LENNIE [*still avoiding being drawn in*]: If you don't want me, you only gotta say so. I'll go right up on them hills and live by myself. And I won't get no mice stole from me.

GEORGE: I want you to stay with me. Jesus Christ, somebody'd shoot you for a coyote if you was by yourself. Stay with me. Your Aunt Clara wouldn't like your runnin' off by yourself, even if she is dead.

LENNIE: George?

GEORGE: Huh?

LENNIE [*craftily*]: Tell me—like you done before.

GEORGE: Tell you what?

LENNIE: About the rabbits.

GEORGE [*near to anger again*]: You ain't gonna put nothing over on me!

LENNIE [*pleading*]: Come on, George . . . tell me! Please! Like you done before.

GEORGE: You get a kick out of that, don't you? All right, I'll tell you. And then we'll lay out our beds and eat our dinner.

LENNIE: Go on, George.

Unrolls his bed and lies on his side, supporting his head on one hand. GEORGE *lays out his bed and sits crosslegged on it.* GEORGE *repeats the next speech rhythmically, as though he had said it many times before.*

GEORGE: Guys like us that work on ranches is the loneliest guys in the world. They ain't got no family. They don't belong no place. They come to a ranch and work up a stake and then they go in to town and blow their stake. And then the first thing you know they're poundin' their tail on some other ranch. They ain't got nothin' to look ahead to.

LENNIE [*delightedly*]: That's it, that's it! Now tell how it is with us.

GEORGE [*still almost chanting*]: With us it ain't like that. We got a future. We got somebody to talk to that gives a damn about us. We don't have to sit in no barroom blowin' in our jack, just because we got no place else to go. If them other guys gets in jail, they can rot for all anybody gives a damn.

LENNIE [*who cannot restrain himself any longer. Bursts into speech*]: But not us! And why? Because . . . because I got you to look after me . . . and you got me to look after you . . . and that's why! [*He laughs.*] Go on, George!

GEORGE: You got it by heart. You can do it yourself.

LENNIE: No, no. I forget some of the stuff. Tell about how it's gonna be.

GEORGE: Some other time.

LENNIE: No, tell how it's gonna be!

GEORGE: Okay. Some day we're gonna get the jack together and we're gonna have a little house, and a couple of acres and a cow and some pigs and . . .

LENNIE [*shouting*]: And live off the fat of the land! And have rabbits. Go on, George! Tell about what we're gonna have in the garden. And about the rabbits in the cages. Tell about the rain in the winter . . . and about the stove and how thick the cream is on the milk, you can hardly cut it. Tell about that, George!

GEORGE: Why don't you do it yourself—you know all of it!

LENNIE: It ain't the same if I tell it. Go on now. How I get to tend the rabbits.

GEORGE [*resignedly*]: Well, we'll have a big vegetable patch and a rabbit hutch and chickens. And when it rains in the winter we'll just say to hell with goin' to work. We'll build up a fire in the stove, and set around it and listen to the rain comin' down on the roof—Nuts! [*Begins to eat with his knife.*] I ain't got time for no more. [*He falls to eating.* LENNIE *imitates him, spilling a few beans from his mouth with every bite.* GEORGE, *gesturing with his knife.*] What you gonna say tomorrow when the boss asks you questions?

LENNIE [*stops chewing in the middle of a bite, swallows painfully. His face contorts with thought*]: I . . . I ain't gonna say a word.

GEORGE: Good boy. That's fine. Say, maybe you're gittin' better. I bet I can let you tend the rabbits . . . specially if you remember as good as that!

LENNIE [*choking with pride*]: I can remember, by God!

GEORGE [*as though remembering something, points his knife at* LENNIE'S *chest*]: Lennie, I want you to look around here. Think you can remember this place? The ranch is 'bout a quarter mile up that way. Just follow the river and you can get here.

LENNIE [*looking around carefully*]: Sure, I can remember here. Didn't I remember 'bout not gonna say a word?

GEORGE: 'Course you did. Well, look, Lennie, if you just happen to get in trouble, I want you to come right here and hide in the brush.

LENNIE [*slowly*]: Hide in the brush.

GEORGE: Hide in the brush until I come for you. Think you can remember that?

LENNIE: Sure I can, George. Hide in the brush till you come for me!

GEORGE: But you ain't gonna get in no trouble. Because if you do I won't let you tend the rabbits.

LENNIE: I won't get in no trouble. I ain't gonna say a word.

GEORGE: You got it. Anyways, I hope so. [GEORGE *stretches out on his blankets. The light dies slowly out of the fire until only the faces of the two men can be seen.* GEORGE *is still eating from his can of beans.*] It's gonna be nice sleeping here. Lookin' up . . . and the leaves . . . Don't build up no more fire. We'll let her die. Jesus, you feel free when you ain't got a job—if you ain't hungry.

They sit silently for a few moments. A night owl is heard far off. From across the river there comes the sound of a coyote howl and on the heels of the howl all the dogs in the country start to bark.

LENNIE [*from almost complete darkness*]: George?

GEORGE: What do you want?

LENNIE: Let's have different color rabbits, George.

GEORGE: Sure. Red rabbits and blue rabbits and green rabbits. Millions of 'em!

LENNIE: Furry ones, George. Like I seen at the fair in Sacramento.

GEORGE: Sure. Furry ones.

LENNIE: 'Cause I can jus' as well go away, George, and live in a cave.

GEORGE [*amiably*]: Aw, shut up.

LENNIE [*after a long pause*]: George?

GEORGE: What is it?

LENNIE: I'm shutting up, George. [*A coyote howls again.*]

CURTAIN

ACT ONE: SCENE II

Late Friday morning.

The interior of a bunkhouse.

Walls, white-washed board and bat. Floors unpainted.

There is a heavy square table with upended boxes around it used for chairs. Over each bunk there is a box nailed to the wall which serves as two shelves on which are the private possessions of the working men.

On top of each bunk there is a large noisy alarm clock ticking madly.

The sun is streaking through the windows. NOTE: *Articles in the boxes on wall are soap, talcum powder, razors, pulp magazines, medicine bottles, combs, and from nails on the sides of the boxes a few neckties.*

There is a hanging light from the ceiling over the table, with a round dim reflector on it.

The curtain rises on an empty stage. Only the ticking of the many alarm clocks is heard.

CANDY, GEORGE *and* LENNIE *are first seen passing the open window of the bunkhouse.*

CANDY: This is the bunkhouse here. Door's around this side. [*The latch on the door rises and* CANDY *enters, a stoop-shouldered old man. He is dressed in blue jeans and a denim coat. He carries a big push broom in his left hand. His right hand is gone at the wrist. He grasps things with his right arm between arm and side. He walks into the room followed by* GEORGE *and* LENNIE. *Conversationally.*] The boss was expecting you last night. He was sore as hell when you wasn't here to go out this morning. [*Points with his handless arm.*] You can have them two beds there.

GEORGE: I'll take the top one . . . I don't want you falling down on me. [*Steps over to the bunk and throws his blankets down. He looks into the nearly empty box shelf over it, then picks up a small yellow can.*] Say, what the hell's this?

CANDY: I don' know.

GEORGE: Says "positively kills lice, roaches and other scourges." What the hell kinda beds you givin' us, anyway? We don't want no pants rabbits.

CANDY [*shifts his broom, holding it between his elbow and his side, takes the can in his left hand and studies the label carefully*]: Tell you what . . . last guy that had this bed was a blacksmith. Helluva nice fellow. Clean a guy as you'd want to meet. Used to wash his hands even *after* he et.

GEORGE [*with gathering anger*]: Then how come he got pillow-pigeons? [LENNIE *puts his blankets on his bunk and sits down, watching* GEORGE *with his mouth slightly open.*]

CANDY: Tell you what. This here blacksmith, name of Whitey, was the kinda guy that would put that stuff around even if there wasn't no bugs. Tell you what he used to do. He'd peel *his* boiled potatoes and take out every little spot before he et it, and if there was a red splotch on an egg, he'd scrape it off. Finally quit about the food. That's the kind of guy Whitey was. Clean. Used to dress up Sundays even when he wasn't goin' no place. Put on a necktie even, and then set in the bunkhouse.

GEORGE [*skeptically*]: I ain't so sure. What da' ya say he quit for?

CANDY [*puts the can in his pocket, rubs his bristly white whiskers with his knuckles*]: Why . . . he just quit the way a guy will. Says it was the food. Didn't give no other reason. Just says "give me my time" one night, the way any guy would. [GEORGE *lifts his bed tick and looks underneath, leans over and inspects the sacking carefully.* LENNIE *does the same with his bed.*]

GEORGE [*half satisfied*]: Well, if there's any grey-backs in this bed, you're gonna hear from me! [*He unrolls his blankets and puts his razor and bar of soap and comb and bottle of pills, his liniment and leather wristband in the box.*]

CANDY: I guess the boss'll be out here in a minute to write your name in. He sure was burned when you wasn't here this morning. Come right in when we was eatin' breakfast and says, "Where the hell's them new men?" He give the stable buck hell, too. Stable buck's a nigger.

GEORGE: Nigger, huh!

CANDY: Yeah. [*Continues.*] Nice fellow too. Got a crooked back where a horse kicked him. Boss gives him hell when he's mad. But the stable buck don't give a damn about that.

GEORGE: What kinda guy is the boss?

CANDY: Well, he's a pretty nice fella for a boss. Gets mad sometimes. But he's pretty nice. Tell you what. Know what he done Christmas? Brung a gallon of whiskey right in here and says, "Drink hearty, boys, Christmas comes but once a year!"

GEORGE: The hell he did! A whole gallon?

CANDY: Yes, sir. Jesus, we had fun! They let the nigger come in that night. Well, sir, a little skinner name Smitty took after the nigger. Done pretty good too. The guys wouldn't let him use his feet so the nigger got him. If he could a used his feet Smitty says he would have killed the nigger. The guys says on account the nigger got a crooked

27

back Smitty can't use his feet. [*He smiles in reverie at the memory.*]

GEORGE: Boss the owner?

CANDY: Naw! Superintendent. Big land company. . . . Yes, sir, that night . . . he come right in here with a whole gallon . . . he set right over there and says, "Drink hearty, boys," . . . he says. . . . [*The door opens. Enter the* BOSS. *He is a stocky man, dressed in blue jean trousers, flannel shirt, a black unbuttoned vest and a black coat. He wears a soiled brown Stetson hat, a pair of high-heeled boots and spurs. Ordinarily he puts his thumbs in his belt.* CANDY, *shuffling towards the door, rubbing his whiskers with his knuckles as he goes.*] Them guys just come. [CANDY *exits and shuts the door behind him.*]

BOSS: I wrote Murray and Ready I wanted two men this morning. You got your work slips?

GEORGE [*digs in his pockets, produces two slips and hands them to the* BOSS]: Here they are.

BOSS [*reading the slips*]: Well, I see it wasn't Murray and Ready's fault. It says right here on the slip, you was to be here for work this morning.

GEORGE: Bus driver give us a bum steer. We had to walk ten miles. That bus driver says we was here when we wasn't. We couldn't thumb no rides. [GEORGE *scowls meaningly at* LENNIE *and* LENNIE *nods to show that he understands.*]

BOSS: Well, I had to send out the grain teams short two buckers. It won't do any good to go out now until after dinner. You'd get lost. [*Pulls out his time book, opens it to where a pencil is stuck between the leaves. Licks his pencil carefully.*] What's your name?

GEORGE: George Milton.

BOSS: George Milton. [*Writing.*] And what's yours?

GEORGE: His name's Lennie Small.

BOSS: Lennie Small. [*Writing.*] Le's see, this is the twentieth. Noon the twentieth. . . . [*Makes positive mark. Closes
the book and puts it in his pocket.*] Where you boys been
workin'?

GEORGE: Up around Weed.

BOSS [*to* LENNIE]: You too?

GEORGE: Yeah. Him too.

BOSS [*to* LENNIE]: Say, you're a big fellow, ain't you?

GEORGE: Yeah, he can work like hell, too.

BOSS: He ain't much of a talker, though, is he?

GEORGE: No, he ain't. But he's a hell of a good worker.
Strong as a bull.

LENNIE [*smiling*]: I'm strong as a bull. [GEORGE *scowls at him
and* LENNIE *drops his head in shame at having forgotten.*]

BOSS [*sharply*]: You are, huh? What can you do?

GEORGE: He can do anything.

BOSS [*addressing* LENNIE]: What can you do? [LENNIE,
looking at GEORGE, *gives a high nervous chuckle.*]

GEORGE [*quickly*]: Anything you tell him. He's a good skinner. He can wrestle grain bags, drive a cultivator. He can
do anything. Just give him a try.

BOSS [*turning to* GEORGE]: Then why don't you let *him*
answer? [LENNIE *laughs.*] What's he laughing about?

GEORGE: He laughs when he gets excited.

BOSS: Yeah?

GEORGE [*loudly*]: But he's a goddamn good worker. I ain't
saying he's bright, because he ain't. But he can put up a
four hundred pound bale.

BOSS [*hooking his thumbs in his belt*]: Say, what you
sellin'?

GEORGE: Huh?

BOSS: I said what stake you got in this guy? You takin' his
pay away from him?

GEORGE: No. Of course I ain't!

BOSS: Yell, I never seen one guy take so much trouble for another guy. I just like to know what your percentage is.

GEORGE: He's my . . . cousin. I told his ole lady I'd take care of him. He got kicked in the head by a horse when he was a kid. He's all right. . . . Just ain't bright. But he can do anything you tell him.

BOSS [*turning half away*]: Well, God knows he don't need no brains to buck barley bags. [*He turns back.*] But don't you try to put nothing over, Milton. I got my eye on you. Why'd you quit in Weed?

GEORGE [*promptly*]: Job was done.

BOSS: What kind of job?

GEORGE: Why . . . we was diggin' a cesspool.

BOSS [*after a pause*]: All right. But don't try to put nothing over 'cause you can't get away with nothing. I seen wise guys before. Go out with the grain teams after dinner. They're out pickin' up barley with the thrashin' machines. Go out with Slim's team.

GEORGE: Slim?

BOSS: Yeah. Big, tall skinner. You'll see him at dinner. [*Up to this time the* BOSS *has been full of business. He has been calm and suspicious. In the following lines he relaxes, but gradually, as though he wanted to talk but felt always the burden of his position. He turns toward the door, but hesitates and allows a little warmth into his manner.*] Been on the road long?

GEORGE [*obviously on guard*]: We was three days in 'Frisco lookin' at the boards.

BOSS [*with heavy jocularity*]: Didn't go to no night clubs, I 'spose?

GEORGE [*stiffly*]: We was lookin' for a job.

BOSS [*attempting to be friendly*]: That's a great town if you got a little jack, 'Frisco.

GEORGE [*refusing to be drawn in*]: We didn't have no jack for nothing like that.

BOSS [*realizes there is no contact to establish; grows rigid with his position again*]: Go out with the grain teams after dinner. When my hands work hard they get pie and when they loaf they bounce down the road on their can. You ask anybody about me. [*He turns and walks out of bunkhouse.*]

GEORGE [*turns to* LENNIE]: So you wasn't gonna say a word! You was gonna leave your big flapper shut. I was gonna do the talkin'. . . . You goddamn near lost us the job!

LENNIE [*stares hopelessly at his hands*]: I forgot.

GEORGE: You forgot. You always forget. Now, he's got his eye on us. Now, we gotta be careful and not make no slips. You keep your big flapper shut after this.

LENNIE: He talked like a kinda nice guy towards the last.

GEORGE [*angrily*]: He's the boss, ain't he? Well, he's the boss first an' a nice guy afterwards. Don't you have nothin' to do with no boss, except do your work and draw your pay. You can't never tell whether you're talkin' to the nice guy or the boss. Just keep your goddamn mouth shut. Then you're all right.

LENNIE: George?

GEORGE: What you want now?

LENNIE: I wasn't kicked in the head with no horse, was I, George?

GEORGE: Be a damn good thing if you was. Save everybody a hell of a lot of trouble!

LENNIE [*flattered*]: You says I was your cousin.

GEORGE: Well, that was a goddamn lie. And I'm glad it was. Why, if I was a relative of yours— [*He stops and listens, then steps to the front door, and looks out.*] Say, what the hell you doin', listenin'?

CANDY [*comes slowly into the room. By a rope, he leads*

an ancient drag-footed, blind sheep dog. Guides it from running into a table leg, with the rope. Sits down on a box, and presses the hind quarters of the old dog down]: Naw ... I wasn't listenin'.... I was just standin' in the shade a minute, scratchin' my dog. I jest now finished swamping out the washhouse.

GEORGE: You was pokin' your big nose into our business! I don't like nosey guys.

CANDY [*looks uneasily from* GEORGE *to* LENNIE *and then back*]: I jest come there ... I didn't hear nothing you guys was sayin'. I ain't interested in nothing you was sayin'. A guy on a ranch don't never listen. Nor he don't ast no questions.

GEORGE [*slightly mollified*]: Damn right he don't! Not if the guy wants to stay workin' long. [*His manner changes.*] That's a helluva ole dog.

CANDY: Yeah. I had him ever since he was a pup. God, he was a good sheep dog, when he was young. [*Rubs his cheek with his knuckles.*] How'd you like the boss?

GEORGE: Pretty good! Seemed all right.

CANDY: He's a nice fella. You got ta take him right, of course. He's runnin' this ranch. He don't take no nonsense.

GEORGE: What time do we eat? Eleven-thirty?

CURLEY *enters. He is dressed in working clothes. He wears brown high-heeled boots and has a glove on his left hand.*

CURLEY: Seen my ole man?

CANDY: He was here just a minute ago, Curley. Went over to the cookhouse, I think.

CURLEY: I'll try to catch him. [*Looking over at the new men, measuring them. Unconsciously bends his elbow and closes his hand and goes into a slight crouch. He walks gingerly close to* LENNIE.] You the new guys my ole man was waitin' for?

GEORGE: Yeah. We just come in.

CURLEY: How's it come you wasn't here this morning?

GEORGE: Got off the bus too soon.

CURLEY [*again addressing* LENNIE]: My ole man got to get the grain out. Ever bucked barley?

GEORGE [*quickly*]: Hell, yes. Done a lot of it.

CURLEY: I mean him. [*To* LENNIE.] Ever bucked barley?

GEORGE: Sure he has.

CURLEY [*irritatedly*]: Let the big guy talk!

GEORGE: 'Spose he don't want ta talk?

CURLEY [*pugnaciously*]: By Christ, he's gotta talk when he's spoke to. What the hell you shovin' into this for?

GEORGE [*stands up and speaks coldly*]: Him and me travel together.

CURLEY: Oh, so it's that way?

GEORGE [*tense and motionless*]: What way?

CURLEY [*letting the subject drop*]: And you won't let the big guy talk? Is that it?

GEORGE: He can talk if he wants to tell you anything. [*He nods slightly to* LENNIE.]

LENNIE [*in a frightened voice*]: We just come in.

CURLEY: Well, next time you answer when you're spoke to, then.

GEORGE: He didn't do nothing to you.

CURLEY [*measuring him*]: You drawin' cards this hand?

GEORGE [*quietly*]: I might.

CURLEY [*stares at him for a moment, his threat moving to the future*]: I'll see you get a chance to ante, anyway. [*He walks out of the room.*]

GEORGE [*after he has made his exit*]: Say, what the hell's he got on his shoulder? Lennie didn't say nothing to him.

CANDY [*looks cautiously at the door*]: That's the Boss's son. Curley's pretty handy. He done quite a bit in the ring. The guys say he's pretty handy.

GEORGE: Well, let 'im be handy. He don't have to take after Lennie. Lennie didn't do nothing to him.

CANDY [*considering*]: Well . . . tell you what, Curley's like a lot a little guys. He hates big guys. He's alla time pickin' scraps with big guys. Kinda like he's mad at 'em because *he* ain't a big guy. You seen little guys like that, ain't you— always scrappy?

GEORGE: Sure, I seen plenty tough little guys. But this here Curley better not make no mistakes about Lennie. Lennie ain't handy, see, but this Curley punk's gonna get hurt if he messes around with Lennie.

CANDY [*skeptically*]: Well, Curley's pretty handy. You know, it never did seem right to me. 'Spose Curley jumps a big guy and licks him. Everybody says what a game guy Curley is. Well, 'spose he jumps 'im and gits licked, everybody says the big guy oughta pick somebody his own size. Seems like Curley ain't givin' nobody a chance.

GEORGE [*watching the door*]: Well, he better watch out for Lennie. Lennie ain't no fighter. But Lennie's strong and quick and Lennie don't know no rules. [*Walks to the square table, and sits down on one of the boxes. Picks up scattered cards and pulls them together and shuffles them.*]

CANDY: Don't tell Curley I said none of this. He'd slough me! He jus' don't give a damn. Won't ever get canned because his ole man's the boss!

GEORGE [*cuts the cards. Turns over and looks at each one as he throws it down*]: This guy Curley sounds like a son-of-a-bitch to me! I don't like mean little guys!

CANDY: Seems to me like he's worse lately. He got married a couple of weeks ago. Wife lives over in the Boss's house. Seems like Curley's worse'n ever since he got married. Like he's settin' on a ant-hill an' a big red ant come up an' nipped 'im on the turnip. Just feels so goddamn miserable he'll strike at anything that moves. I'm kinda sorry for 'im.

GEORGE: Maybe he's showin' off for his wife.

CANDY: You seen that glove on his left hand?

GEORGE: Sure I seen it!

CANDY: Well, that glove's full of vaseline.

GEORGE: Vaseline? What the hell for?

CANDY: Curley says he's keepin' that hand soft for his wife.

GEORGE: That's a dirty kind of a thing to tell around.

CANDY: I ain't quite so sure. I seen such funny things a guy will do to try to be nice. I ain't sure. But you jus' wait till you see Curley's wife!

GEORGE [*begins to lay out a solitaire hand, speaks casually*]: Is she purty?

CANDY: Yeah. Purty, but—

GEORGE [*studying his cards*]: But what?

CANDY: Well, she got the eye.

GEORGE [*still playing at his solitaire hand*]: Yeah? Married two weeks an' got the eye? Maybe that's why Curley's pants is fulla ants.

CANDY: Yes, sir, I seen her give Slim the eye. Slim's a jerk-line skinner. Hell of a nice fella. Well, I seen her give Slim the eye. Curley never seen it. And I seen her give a skinner named Carlson the eye.

GEORGE [*pretending a very mild interest*]: Looks like we was gonna have fun!

CANDY [*stands up*]: Know what I think? [*Waits for an answer. George doesn't answer.*] Well, I think Curley's married himself a tart.

GEORGE [*casually*]: He ain't the first. Black queen on a red king. Yes, sir . . . there's plenty done that!

CANDY [*moves towards the door, leading his dog out with him*]: I got to be settin' out the wash basins for the guys. The teams'll be in before long. You guys gonna buck barley?

GEORGE: Yeah.

CANDY: You won't tell Curley nothing I said?

GEORGE: Hell, no!

CANDY [*just before he goes out the door, he turns back*]: Well, you look her over, mister. You see if she ain't a tart! [*He exits.*]

GEORGE [*continuing to play out his solitaire. He turns to* LENNIE]: Look, Lennie, this here ain't no set-up. You gonna have trouble with that Curley guy. I seen that kind before. You know what he's doin'. He's kinda feelin' you out. He figures he's got you scared. And he's gonna take a sock at you, first chance he gets.

LENNIE [*frightened*]: I don't want no trouble. Don't let him sock me, George!

GEORGE: I hate them kind of bastards. I seen plenty of 'em. Like the ole guy says: "Curley don't take no chances. He always figures to win." [*Thinks for a moment.*] If he tangles with you, Lennie, we're goin' get the can. Don't make no mistake about that. He's the Boss's kid. Look, you try to keep away from him, will you? Don't never speak to him. If he comes in here you move clear to the other side of the room. Will you remember that, Lennie?

LENNIE [*mourning*]: I don't want no trouble. I never done nothing to him!

GEORGE: Well, that won't do you no good, if Curley wants to set himself up for a fighter. Just don't have nothing to do with him. Will you remember?

LENNIE: Sure, George . . . I ain't gonna say a word.

Sounds of the teams coming in from the fields, jingling of harness, croak of heavy laden axles, men talking to and cussing the horses. Crack of a whip and from a distance a voice calling.

SLIM'S VOICE: Stable buck! Hey! Stable buck!

GEORGE: Here come the guys. Just don't say nothing.

LENNIE [*timidly*]: You ain't mad, George?

GEORGE: I ain't mad at you. I'm mad at this here Curley bastard! I wanted we should get a little stake together. Maybe a hundred dollars. You keep away from Curley.

LENNIE: Sure I will. I won't say a word.

GEORGE [*hesitating*]: Don't let 'im pull you in—but—if the son-of-a-bitch socks you—let him have it!

LENNIE: Let him have what, George?

GEORGE: Never mind. . . . Look, if you get in any kind of trouble, you remember what I told you to do.

LENNIE: If I get in any trouble, you ain't gonna let me tend the rabbits?

GEORGE: That's not what I mean. You remember where we slept last night. Down by the river?

LENNIE: Oh, sure I remember. I go there and hide in the brush until you come for me.

GEORGE: That's it. Hide till I come for you. Don't let nobody see you. Hide in the brush by the river. Now say that over.

LENNIE: Hide in the brush by the river. Down in the brush by the river.

GEORGE: If you get in trouble.

LENNIE: If I get in trouble.

A brake screeches outside and a call: "Stable buck, oh, stable buck!" "Where the hell's that goddamn nigger?" Suddenly CURLEY'S WIFE *is standing in the door. Full, heavily rouged lips. Wide-spaced, made-up eyes, her fingernails are bright red, her hair hangs in little rolled clusters like sausages. She wears a cotton house dress and red mules, on the insteps of which are little bouquets of red ostrich feathers.* GEORGE *and* LENNIE *look up at her.*

CURLEY'S WIFE: I'm lookin' for Curley!

GEORGE [*looks away from her*]: He was in here a minute ago but he went along.

CURLEY'S WIFE [*puts her hands behind her back and leans against the door frame so that her body is thrown forward*]: You're the new fellas that just come, ain't you?

GEORGE [*sullenly*]: Yeah.

CURLEY'S WIFE [*bridles a little and inspects her fingernails*]: Sometimes Curley's in here.

GEORGE [*brusquely*]: Well, he ain't now!

CURLEY'S WIFE [*playfully*]: Well, if he ain't, I guess I'd better look some place else. [LENNIE *watches her, fascinated.*]

GEORGE: If I see Curley I'll pass the word you was lookin' for him.

CURLEY'S WIFE: Nobody can't blame a person for lookin'.

GEORGE: That depends what she's lookin' for.

CURLEY'S WIFE [*a little wearily, dropping her coquetry*]: I'm jus' lookin' for somebody to talk to. Don't you never jus' want to talk to somebody?

SLIM [*offstage*]: Okay! Put that lead pair in the north stalls.

CURLEY'S WIFE [*to* SLIM, *offstage*]: Hi, Slim!

SLIM [*voice offstage*]: Hello.

CURLEY'S WIFE: I—I'm tryin' to find Curley.

SLIM'S VOICE [*offstage*]: Well, you ain't tryin' very hard. I seen him goin' in your house.

CURLEY'S WIFE [*turning back toward* GEORGE *and* LENNIE]: I gotta be goin'! [*She exits hurriedly.*]

GEORGE [*looking around at* LENNIE]: Jesus, what a tramp! So, that's what Curley picks for a wife. God Almighty, did you smell that stink she's got on? I can still smell her. Don't have to see *her* to know she's around.

LENNIE: She's purty!

GEORGE: Yeah. And she's sure hidin' it. Curley got his work ahead of him.

LENNIE [*still staring at the doorway where she was*]: Gosh, she's purty!

GEORGE [*turning furiously at him*]: Listen to me, you crazy bastard. Don't you even look at that bitch. I don't care what she says or what she does. I seen 'em poison before, but I ain't never seen no piece of jail bait worse than her. Don't you even smell near her!

LENNIE: I never smelled, George!

GEORGE: No, you never. But when she was standin' there showin' her legs, you wasn't lookin' the other way neither!

LENNIE: I never meant no bad things, George. Honest I never.

GEORGE: Well, you keep away from her. You let Curley take the rap. He let himself in for it. [*Disgustedly.*] Glove full of vaseline. I bet he's eatin' raw eggs and writin' to patent-medicine houses.

LENNIE [*cries out*]: I don't like this place. This ain't no good place. I don't like this place!

GEORGE: Listen—I don't like it here no better than you do. But we gotta keep it till we get a stake. We're flat. We gotta get a stake. [*Goes back to the table, thoughtfully.*] If we can get just a few dollars in the poke we'll shove off and go up to the American River and pan gold. Guy can make a couple dollars a day there.

LENNIE [*eagerly*]: Let's go, George. Let's get out of here. It's mean here.

GEORGE [*shortly*]: I tell you we gotta stay a little while. We gotta get a stake. [*The sounds of running water and rattle of basins are heard.*] Shut up now, the guys'll be comin' in! [*Pensively.*] Maybe we ought to wash up. . . . But hell, we ain't done nothin' to get dirty.

SLIM [*enters. He is a tall, dark man in blue jeans and a short denim jacket. He carries a crushed Stetson hat under his arm and combs his long dark damp hair straight back.*

He stands and moves with a kind of majesty. He finishes combing his hair. Smoothes out his crushed hat, creases it in the middle and puts it on. In a gentle voice]: It's brighter'n a bitch outside. Can't hardly see nothing in here. You the new guys?

GEORGE: Just come.

SLIM: Goin' to buck barley?

GEORGE: That's what the boss says.

SLIM: Hope you get on my team.

GEORGE: Boss said we'd go with a jerk-line skinner named Slim.

SLIM: That's me.

GEORGE: You a jerk-line skinner?

SLIM [*in self-disparagement*]: I can snap 'em around a little.

GEORGE [*terribly impressed*]: That kinda makes you Jesus Christ on this ranch, don't it?

SLIM [*obviously pleased*]: Oh, nuts!

GEORGE [*chuckles*]: Like the man says, "The boss tells you what to do. But if you want to know how to do it, you got to ask the mule skinner." The man says any guy that can drive twelve Arizona jack rabbits with a jerk line can fall in a toilet and come up with a mince pie under each arm.

SLIM [*laughing*]: Well, I hope you get on my team. I got a pair a punks that don't know a barley bag from a blue ball. You guys ever bucked any barley?

GEORGE: Hell, yes. I ain't nothin' to scream about, but that big guy there can put up more grain alone than most pairs can.

SLIM [*looks approvingly at* GEORGE]: You guys travel around together?

GEORGE: Sure. We kinda look after each other. [*Points at* LENNIE *with his thumb.*] He ain't bright. Hell of a good worker, though. Hell of a nice fella too. I've knowed him for a long time.

SLIM: Ain't many guys travel around together. I don't know why. Maybe everybody in the whole damn world is scared of each other.

GEORGE: It's a lot nicer to go 'round with a guy you know. You get used to it an' then it ain't no fun alone any more. [*Enter* CARLSON. *Big-stomached, powerful man. His head still drips water from scrubbing and dousing.*]

CARLSON: Hello, Slim! [*He looks at* GEORGE *and* LENNIE.]

SLIM: These guys just come.

CARLSON: Glad to meet ya! My name's Carlson.

GEORGE: I'm George Milton. This here's Lennie Small.

CARLSON: Glad to meet you. He ain't very small. [*Chuckles at his own joke.*] He ain't small at all. Meant to ask you, Slim, how's your bitch? I seen she wasn't under your wagon this morning.

SLIM: She slang her pups last night. Nine of 'em. I drownded four of 'em right off. She couldn't feed that many.

CARLSON: Got five left, huh?

SLIM: Yeah. Five. I kep' the biggest.

CARLSON: What kinda dogs you think they gonna be?

SLIM: I don't know. Some kind of shepherd, I guess. That's the most kind I seen around here when she's in heat.

CARLSON [*laughs*]: I had an airedale an' a guy down the road got one of them little white floozy dogs, well, she was in heat and the guy locks her up. But my airedale, named Tom he was, he et a woodshed clear down to the roots to get to her. Guy come over one day, he's sore as hell, he says, "I wouldn't mind if my bitch had pups, but Christ Almighty, this morning she slang a litter of Shetland ponies. . . ." [*Takes off his hat and scratches his head.*] Got five pups, huh! Gonna keep all of 'em?

SLIM: I don' know, gotta keep 'em awhile, so they can drink Lulu's milk.

CARLSON [*thoughtfully*]: Well, looka here, Slim, I been

thinkin'. That dog of Candy's is so goddamn old he can't hardly walk. Stinks like hell. Every time Candy brings him in the bunkhouse, I can smell him two or three days. Why don't you get Candy to shoot his ol' dog, and give him one of them pups to raise up? I can smell that dog a mile off. Got no teeth. Can't eat. Candy feeds him milk. He can't chew nothing else. And leadin' him around on a string so he don't bump into things . . . [*The triangle outside begins to ring wildly. Continues for a few moments, then stops suddenly.*] There she goes! [*Outside there is a burst of voices as a group of men go by.*]

SLIM [*to* LENNIE *and* GEORGE]: You guys better come on while they's still somethin' to eat. Won't be nothing left in a couple of minutes. [*Exit* SLIM *and* CARLSON, LENNIE *watches* GEORGE *excitedly.*]

LENNIE: George!

GEORGE [*rumpling his cards into a pile*]: Yeah, I heard 'im, Lennie . . . I'll ask 'im!

LENNIE [*excitedly*]: A brown and white one.

GEORGE: Come on, let's get dinner. I don't know whether he's got a brown and white one.

LENNIE: You ask him right away, George, so he won't kill no more of 'em!

GEORGE: Sure! Come on now—le's go. [*They start for the door.*]

CURLEY [*bounces in, angrily*]: You seen a girl around here?

GEORGE [*coldly*]: 'Bout half an hour ago, mebbe.

CURLEY: Well, what the hell was she doin'?

GEORGE [*insultingly*]: She *said* she was lookin' for you.

CURLEY [*measures both men with his eyes for a moment*]: Which way did she go?

GEORGE: I don't know. I didn't watch her go. [CURLEY *scowls at him a moment and then turns and hurries out the door.*] You know, Lennie, I'm scared I'm gonna tangle

with that bastard myself. I hate his guts! Jesus Christ,
come on! They won't be a damn thing left to eat.

LENNIE: Will you ask him about a brown and white one?
[*They exeunt.*]

CURTAIN

ACT TWO

ACT TWO: SCENE I

About seven-thirty Friday evening.

Same bunkhouse interior as in last scene.

The evening light is seen coming in through the window, but it is quite dark in the interior of the bunkhouse.

From outside comes the sound of a horseshoe game. Thuds on the dirt and occasional clangs as a shoe hits the peg. Now and then voices are raised in approval or derision: "That's a good one."... "Goddamn right it's a good one."... "Here goes for a ringer. I need a ringer."... "Goddamn near got it, too."

SLIM *and* GEORGE *come into the darkening bunkhouse together.* SLIM *reaches up and turns on the tin-shaded electric light. Sits down on a box at the table.* GEORGE *takes his place opposite.*

SLIM: It wasn't nothing. I would of had to drown most of them pups anyway. No need to thank me about that.

GEORGE: Wasn't much to you, mebbe, but it was a hell of a lot to him. Jesus Christ, I don't know how we're gonna get him to sleep in here. He'll want to stay right out in the barn. We gonna have trouble keepin' him from gettin' right in the box with them pups.

SLIM: Say, you sure was right about him. Maybe he ain't bright—but I never seen such a worker. He damn near killed his partner buckin' barley. He'd take his end of that sack—[*a gesture*]—pretty near kill his partner. God Almighty, I never seen such a strong guy.

GEORGE [*proudly*]: You just tell Lennie what to do and he'll do it if it don't take no figuring.

Outside the sound of the horseshoe game goes on: "Son of a bitch if I can win a goddamn game." . . . "Me neither. You'd think them shoes was anvils."

SLIM: Funny how you and him string along together.

GEORGE: What's so funny about it?

SLIM: Oh, I don't know. Hardly none of the guys ever travels around together. I hardly never seen two guys travel together. You know how the hands are. They come in and get their bunk and work a month and then they quit and go on alone. Never seem to give a damn about nobody. Jest seems kinda funny. A cuckoo like him and a smart guy like you traveling together.

GEORGE: I ain't so bright neither or I wouldn't be buckin' barley for my fifty and found. If I was bright, if I was even a little bit smart, I'd have my own place and I'd be bringin' in my own crops 'stead of doin' all the work and not gettin' what comes up out of the ground. [*He falls silent for a moment.*]

SLIM: A guy'd like to do that. Sometime I'd like to cuss a string of mules that was my own mules.

GEORGE: It ain't so funny, him and me goin' round together. Him and me was both born in Auburn. I knowed his aunt. She took him when he was a baby and raised him up. When his aunt died Lennie jus' come along with me, out workin'. Got kinda used to each other after a little while.

SLIM: Uh huh.

GEORGE: First I used to have a hell of a lot of fun with him. Used to play jokes on him because he was too dumb to take care of himself. But, hell, he was too dumb even to know when he had a joke played on him. [*Sarcastically.*]

Hell, yes, I had fun! Made me seem goddamn smart along-side of him.

SLIM: I seen it that way.

GEORGE: Why, he'd do any damn thing I tole him. If I tole him to walk over a cliff, over he'd go. You know that wasn't so damn much fun after a while. He never got mad about it, neither. I've beat hell out of him and he could bust every bone in my body jest with his hands. But he never lifted a finger against me.

SLIM [*braiding a bull whip*]: Even if you socked him, wouldn't he?

GEORGE: No, by God! I tell you what made me stop play-ing jokes. One day a bunch of guys was standin' aroun' up on the Sacramento River. I was feelin' pretty smart. I turns to Lennie and I says, "Jump in."

SLIM: What happened?

GEORGE: He jumps. Couldn't swim a stroke. He damn near drowned. And he was so nice to me for pullin' him out. Clean forgot I tole him to jump in. Well, I ain't done nothin' like that no more. Makes me kinda sick tellin' about it.

SLIM: He's a nice fella. A guy don't need no sense to be a nice fella. Seems to be sometimes it's jest the other way round. Take a real smart guy, he ain't hardly ever a nice fella.

GEORGE [*stacking the scattered cards and getting his soli-taire game ready again*]: I ain't got no people. I seen guys that go round on the ranches alone. That ain't no good. They don't have no fun. After a while they get mean.

SLIM [*quietly*]: Yeah, I seen 'em get mean. I seen 'em get so they don't want to talk to nobody. Some ways they got to. You take a bunch of guys all livin' in one room an' by God they got to mind their own business. 'Bout the only private thing a guy's got is where he come from and where he's goin'.

GEORGE: 'Course Lennie's a goddamn nuisance most of the time. But you get used to goin' round with a guy and you can't get rid of him. I mean you get used to him an' you can't get rid of bein' used to him. I'm sure drippin' at the mouth. I ain't told nobody all this before.

SLIM: Do you want to git rid of him?

GEORGE: Well, he gets in trouble all the time. Because he's so goddamn dumb. Like what happened in Weed. [*He stops, alarmed at what he has said.*] You wouldn't tell nobody?

SLIM [*calmly*]: What did he do in Weed?

GEORGE: You wouldn't tell?—No, course you wouldn't.

SLIM: What did he do?

GEORGE: Well, he seen this girl in a red dress. Dumb bastard like he is he wants to touch everything he likes. Jest wants to feel of it. So he reaches out to feel this red dress. Girl lets out a squawk and that gets Lennie all mixed up. He holds on 'cause that's the only thing he can think to do.

SLIM: The hell!

GEORGE: Well, this girl squawks her head off. I'm right close and I hear all the yellin', so I comes a-running. By that time Lennie's scared to death. You know, I had to sock him over the head with a fence picket to make him let go.

SLIM: So what happens then?

GEORGE [*carefully building his solitaire hand*]: Well, she runs in and tells the law she's been raped. The guys in Weed start out to lynch Lennie. So there we sit in an irrigation ditch, under water all the rest of that day. Got only our heads sticking out of water, up under the grass that grows out of the side of the ditch. That night we run outa there.

SLIM: Didn't hurt the girl none, huh?

GEORGE: Hell no, he jes' scared her.

SLIM: He's a funny guy.

GEORGE: Funny! Why, one time, you know what that big baby done! He was walking along a road—[*Enter* LEN-NIE *through the door. He wears his coat over his shoulder like a cape and walks hunched over.*] Hi, Lennie. How do you like your pup?

LENNIE [*breathlessly*]: He's brown and white jus' like I wanted. [*Goes directly to his bunk and lies down. Face to the wall and knees drawn up.*]

GEORGE [*puts down his cards deliberately*]: Lennie!

LENNIE [*over his shoulder*]: Huh? What you want George?

GEORGE [*sternly*]: I tole ya, ya couldn't bring that pup in here.

LENNIE: What pup, George? I ain't got no pup.

GEORGE *goes quickly over to him, grabs him by the shoulder and rolls him over. He picks up a tiny puppy from where* LENNIE *has been concealing it against his stomach.*

LENNIE [*quickly*]: Give him to me, George.

GEORGE: You get right up and take this pup to the nest. He's got to sleep with his mother. Ya want ta kill him? Jes' born last night and ya take him out of the nest. Ya take him back or I'll tell Slim not to let you have him.

LENNIE [*pleadingly*]: Give him to me, George. I'll take him back. I didn't mean no bad thing, George. Honest I didn't. I jus' want to pet him a little.

GEORGE [*giving the pup to him*]: All right, you get him back there quick. And don't you take him out no more. [LENNIE *scuttles out of the room.*]

SLIM: Jesus, he's just like a kid, ain't he?

GEORGE: Sure he's like a kid. There ain't no more harm in him than a kid neither, except he's so strong. I bet he won't come in here to sleep tonight. He'll sleep right alongside that box in the barn. Well, let him. He ain't doin' no harm out there. [*The light has faded out outside and it appears quite dark outside. Enter* CANDY *leading his old dog by a string.*]

CANDY: Hello, Slim. Hello, George. Didn't neither of you play horseshoes?

SLIM: I don't like to play every night.

CANDY [*goes to his bunk and sits down, presses the old blind dog to the floor beside him*]: Either you guys got a slug of whiskey? I got a gut ache.

SLIM: I ain't. I'd drink it myself if I had. And I ain't got no gut ache either.

CANDY: Goddamn cabbage give it to me. I knowed it was goin' to before I ever et it. [*Enter* CARLSON *and* WHIT.]

CARLSON: Jesus, how that nigger can pitch shoes!

SLIM: He's plenty good.

WHIT: Damn right he is.

CARLSON: Yeah. He don't give nobody else a chance to win. [*Stops and sniffs the air. Looks around until he sees* CANDY'S *dog.*] God Almighty, that dog stinks. Get him outa here, Candy. I don't know nothing that stinks as bad as ole dogs. You got to get him outa here.

CANDY [*lying down on his bunk, reaches over and pats the ancient dog, speaks softly*]: I been round him so much I never notice how he stinks.

CARLSON: Well, I can't stand him in here. That stink hangs round even after he's gone. [*Walks over and stands looking down at the dog.*] Got no teeth. All stiff with rheumatism. He ain't no good to you, Candy. Why don't you shoot him?

CANDY [*uncomfortably*]: Well, hell, I had him so long! Had him since he was a pup. I herded sheep with him. [*Proudly.*] You wouldn't think it to look at him now. He was the best damn sheep dog I ever seen.

GEORGE: I knowed a guy in Weed that had an airedale that could herd sheep. Learned it from the other dogs.

CARLSON [*sticking to his point*]: Lookit, Candy. This ole dog jus' suffers itself all the time. If you was to take him out and shoot him—right in the back of the head ... [*Leans over and points.*] ... right there, why he never'd know what hit him.

CANDY [*unhappily*]: No, I couldn't do that. I had him too long.

CARLSON [*insisting*]: He don't have no fun no more. He stinks like hell. Tell you what I'll do. I'll shoot him for you. Then it won't be you that done it.

CANDY [*sits up on the bunk, rubbing his whiskers nervously, speaks plaintively*]: I had him from a pup.

WHIT: Let 'im alone, Carl. It ain't a guy's dog that matters. It's the way the guy feels about the dog. Hell, I had a mutt once I wouldn't a traded for a field trial pointer.

CARLSON [*being persuasive*]: Well, Candy ain't being nice to him, keeping him alive. Lookit, Slim's bitch got a litter right now. I bet you Slim would give ya one of them pups to raise up, wouldn't ya, Slim?

SLIM [*studying the dog*]: Yeah. You can have a pup if you want to.

CANDY [*helplessly*]: Mebbe it would hurt. [*After a moment's pause, positively.*] And I don't mind taking care of him.

CARLSON: Aw, he'd be better off dead. The way I'd shoot him he wouldn't feel nothin'. I'd put the gun right there. [*Points with his toe.*] Right back of the head.

WHIT: Aw, let 'im alone, Carl.

CARLSON: Why, hell, he wouldn't even quiver.

WHIT: Let 'im alone. [*He produces a magazine.*] Say, did you see this? Did you see this in the book here?

CARLSON: See what?

WHIT: Right there. Read that.

CARLSON: I don't want to read nothing. . . . It'd be all over in a minute, Candy. Come on.

WHIT: Did you see it, Slim? Go on, read it. Read it out loud.

SLIM: What is it?

WHIT: Read it.

SLIM [*reads slowly*]: "Dear Editor: I read your mag for six years and I think it is the best on the market. I like stories by Peter Rand. I think he is a whing-ding. Give us more like the Dark Rider. I don't write many letters. Just thought I would tell you I think your mag is the best dime's worth I ever spen'." [*Looks up questioningly.*] What you want me to read that for?

WHIT: Go on, read the name at the bottom.

SLIM [*reading*]: "Yours for Success, William Tenner." [*Looks up at* WHIT.] What ya want me to read that for?

CARLSON: Come on, Candy—what you say?

WHIT [*taking the magazine and closing it impressively. Talks to cover* CARLSON]: You don't remember Bill Tenner? Worked here about three months ago?

SLIM [*thinking*]: Little guy? Drove a cultivator?

WHIT: That's him. That's the guy.

CARLSON [*has refused to be drawn into this conversation*]: Look, Candy. If you want me to, I'll put the old devil outa his misery right now and get it over with. There ain't nothin' left for him. Can't eat, can't see, can't hardly walk. Tomorrow you can pick one of Slim's pups.

SLIM: Sure . . . I got a lot of 'em.

CANDY [*hopefully*]: You ain't got no gun.

CARLSON: The hell, I ain't. Got a Luger. It won't hurt him none at all.

CANDY: Mebbe tomorrow. Let's wait till tomorrow.

CARLSON: I don't see no reason for it. [*Goes to his bunk, pulls a bag from underneath, takes a Luger pistol out.*] Let's get it over with. We can't sleep with him stinking around in here. [*He snaps a shell into the chamber, sets the safety and puts the pistol into his hip pocket.*]

SLIM [*as* Candy *looks toward him for help*]: Better let him go, Candy.

CANDY [*looks at each person for some hope.* WHIT *makes a gesture of protest and then resigns himself. The others look away, to avoid responsibility. At last, very softly and hopelessly*]: All right. Take him.

He doesn't look down at the dog at all. Lies back on his bunk and crosses his arms behind his head and stares at the ceiling. CARLSON *picks up the string, helps the dog to its feet.*

CARLSON: Come, boy. Come on, boy. [*To* CANDY, *apologetically.*] He won't even feel it. [CANDY *does not move nor answer him.*] Come on, boy. That's the stuff. Come on. [*He leads the dog toward the door.*]

SLIM: Carlson?

CARLSON: Yeah.

SLIM [*curtly*]: Take a shovel.

CARLSON: Oh, sure, I get you.

Exit CARLSON *with the dog.* GEORGE *follows to the door, shuts it carefully and sets the latch.* CANDY *lies rigidly on his bunk. The next scene is one of silence and quick staccato speeches.*

SLIM [*loudly*]: One of my lead mules got a bad hoof. Got to get some tar on it. [*There is a silence.*]

GEORGE [*loudly*]: Anybody like to play a little euchre?

WHIT: I'll lay out a few with you.

They take places opposite each other at the table but GEORGE *does not shuffle the cards. He ripples the edge of the deck. Everybody looks over at him. He stops. Silence again.*

SLIM [*compassionately*]: Candy, you can have any of them pups you want. [*There is no answer from* CANDY. *There is a little gnawing noise on the stage.*]

GEORGE: Sounds like there was a rat under there. We ought to set a trap there. [*Deep silence again.*]

WHIT [*exasperated*]: What the hell is takin' him so long? Lay out some cards, why don't you? We ain't gonna get no euchre played this way.

GEORGE *studies the backs of the cards. And after a long silence there is a shot in the distance. All the men start a bit, look quickly at* CANDY. *For a moment he continues to stare at the ceiling and then rolls slowly over and faces the wall.* GEORGE *shuffles the cards noisily and deals them.*

GEORGE: Well, let's get to it.

WHIT [*still to cover the moment*]: Yeah . . . I guess you guys really come here to work, huh?

GEORGE: How do you mean?

WHIT [*chuckles*]: Well, you come on a Friday. You got two days to work till Sunday.

GEORGE: I don't see how you figure.

WHIT: You do if you been round these big ranches much. A guy that wants to look over a ranch comes in Saturday afternoon. He gets Saturday night supper, three meals on Sunday and he can quit Monday morning after breakfast without turning a hand. But you come to work on Friday noon. You got ta put in a day and a half no matter how ya figure it.

GEORGE [*quietly*]: We're goin' stick around awhile. Me and Lennie's gonna roll up a stake. [*Door opens and the Negro stable buck puts in his head. A lean-faced Negro with pained eyes.*]

CROOKS: Mr. Slim.

SLIM [*who has been watching* CANDY *the whole time*]: Huh? Oh, hello, Crooks, what's the matter?

CROOKS: You tole me to warm up tar for that mule's foot. I got it warm now.

SLIM: Oh, sure, Crooks. I'll come right out and put it on.

CROOKS: I can do it for you if you want, Mr. Slim.

SLIM [*standing up*]: Naw, I'll take care of my own team.

CROOKS: Mr. Slim.

SLIM: Yeah.

CROOKS: That big new guy is messing round your pups in the barn.

SLIM: Well, he ain't doin' no harm. I give him one of them pups.

CROOKS: Just thought I'd tell ya. He's takin' 'em out of the nest and handling 'em. That won't do 'em no good.

SLIM: Oh, he won't hurt 'em.

GEORGE [*looks up from his cards*]: If that crazy bastard is foolin' round too much jus' kick him out. [SLIM *follows the stable buck out.*]

WHIT [*examining his cards*]: Seen the new kid yet?

GEORGE: What kid?

WHIT: Why, Curley's new wife.

GEORGE [*cautiously*]: Yeah, I seen her.

WHIT: Well, ain't she a lulu?

GEORGE: I ain't seen that much of her.

WHIT: Well, you stick around and keep your eyes open. You'll see plenty of her. I never seen nobody like her. She's just workin' on everybody all the time. Seems like she's even workin' on the stable buck. I don't know what the hell she wants.

GEORGE [*casually*]: Been any trouble since she got here? [*Obviously neither man is interested in the card game.* WHIT *lays down his hand and* GEORGE *gathers the cards in and lays out a solitaire hand.*]

WHIT: I see what you mean. No, they ain't been no trouble yet. She's only been here a couple of weeks. Curley's got yellow jackets in his drawers, but that's all so far. Every time the guys is around she shows up. She's lookin' for Curley. Or she thought she left somethin' layin' around and she's lookin' for that. Seems like she can't keep away from guys. And Curley's runnin' round like a cat lookin' for a dirt road. But they ain't been no trouble.

GEORGE: Ranch with a bunch of guys on it ain't no place for a girl. Specially like her.

WHIT: If she's give you any ideas you ought to come in town with us guys tomorrow night.

GEORGE: Why, what's doin'?

WHIT: Just the usual thing. We go in to old Susy's place. Hell of a nice place. Old Susy is a laugh. Always cracking jokes. Like she says when we come up on the front porch last Saturday night: Susy opens the door and she yells over her shoulder: "Get your coats on, girls, here comes the sheriff." She never talks dirty neither. Got five girls there.

GEORGE: What does it set you back?

WHIT: Two and a half. You can get a shot of whiskey for fifteen cents. Susy got nice chairs to set in too. If a guy don't want to flop, why, he can just set in them chairs and have a couple or three shots and just pass the time of day. Susy don't give a damn. She ain't rushin' guys through, or kicking them out if they don't want to flop.

GEORGE: Might go in and look the joint over.

WHIT: Sure. Come along. It's a hell of a lot of fun—her crackin' jokes all the time. Like she says one time, she says: "I've knew people that if they got a rag rug on the floor and a kewpie doll lamp on the phonograph they think they're runnin' a parlor house." That's Gladys's house she's talkin' about. And Susy says: "I know what you boys want," she says: "My girls is clean," she says. "And there ain't no water in my whiskey," she says. "If any you guys want to look at a kewpie doll lamp and take your chance of gettin' burned, why, you know where to go."

She says: "They's guys round here walkin' bowlegged because they liked to look at a kewpie doll lamp."

GEORGE: Gladys runs the other house, huh?

WHIT: Yeah. [*Enter* CARLSON. CANDY *looks at him.*]

CARLSON: God, it's a dark night. [*Goes to his bunk; starts cleaning his pistol.*]

WHIT: We don't never go to Gladys's. Gladys gits three bucks, and two bits a shot and she don't crack no jokes. But Susy's place is clean and she got nice chairs. A guy can set in there like he lived there. Don't let no Manila Goo-Goos in, neither.

GEORGE: Aw, I don't know. Me and Lennie's rollin' up a stake. I might go in and set and have a shot, but I ain't puttin' out no two and a half.

WHIT: Well, a guy got to have some fun sometimes. [*Enter* LENNIE. LENNIE *creeps to his bunk and sits down.*]

GEORGE: Didn't bring him back in, did you, Lennie?

LENNIE: No, George, honest I didn't. See?

WHIT: Say, how about this euchre game?

GEORGE: Okay. I didn't think you wanted to play. [*Enter* CURLEY *excitedly.*]

CURLEY: Any you guys seen my wife?

WHIT: She ain't been here.

CURLEY [*looks theateningly about the room*]: Where the hell's Slim?

GEORGE: Went out in the barn. He was goin' put some tar on a split hoof.

CURLEY: How long ago did he go?

GEORGE: Oh, five, ten miutes. [CURLEY *jumps out the door.*]

WHIT [*standing up*]: I guess maybe I'd like to see this. Curley must be spoilin' or he wouldn't start for Slim. Curley's handy, goddamn handy. But just the same he better leave Slim alone.

GEORGE: Thinks Slim's with his wife, don't he?

WHIT: Looks like it. 'Course Slim ain't. Least I don't think Slim is. But I like to see the fuss if it comes off. Come on, le's go.

GEORGE: I don't want to git mixed up in nothing. Me and Lennie got to make a stake.

CARLSON [*finishes cleaning gun, puts it in his bag and stands up*]: I'll look her over. Ain't seen a good fight in a hell of a while. [WHIT *and* CARLSON *exeunt.*]

GEORGE: You see Slim out in the barn?

LENNIE: Sure. He tole me I better not pet that pup no more, like I said.

GEORGE: Did you see that girl out there?

LENNIE: You mean Curley's girl?

GEORGE: Yeah. Did she come in the barn?

LENNIE [*cautiously*]: No—anyways I never seen her.

GEORGE: You never seen Slim talkin' to her?

LENNIE: Uh-uh. She ain't been in the barn.

GEORGE: Okay. I guess them guys ain't gonna see no fight. If they's any fightin', Lennie, ya get out of the way and stay out.

LENNIE: I don't want no fight. [George *lays out his solitaire hand.* LENNIE *picks up a face card and studies it. Turns it over and studies it again.*] Both ends the same. George, why is it both ends the same?

GEORGE: I don't know. That jus' the way they make 'em. What was Slim doin' in the barn when you seen him?

LENNIE: Slim?

GEORGE: Sure, you seen him in the barn. He tole you not to pet the pups so much.

LENNIE: Oh. Yeah. He had a can of tar and a paint brush. I don't know what for.

GEORGE: You sure that girl didn't come in like she come in here today?

LENNIE: No, she never come.

GEORGE [*sighs*]: You give me a good whorehouse every time. A guy can go in and get drunk and get it over all at once and no messes. And he knows how much it's goin' set him back. These tarts is jus' buckshot to a guy. [LENNIE *listens with admiration, moving his lips, and* GEORGE *continues.*] You remember Andy Cushman, Lennie? Went to grammar school same time as us?

LENNIE: The one that his ole lady used to make hot cakes for the kids?

GEORGE: Yeah. That's the one. You can remember if they's somepin' to eat in it. [*Scores up some cards in his solitaire playing.*] Well, Andy's in San Quentin right now on account of a tart.

LENNIE: George?

GEORGE: Huh?

LENNIE: How long is it goin' be till we git that little place to live on the fat of the land?

GEORGE: I don't know. We gotta get a big stake together. I know a little place we can get cheap, but they ain't givin' it away. [CANDY *turns slowly over and watches* GEORGE.]

LENNIE: Tell about that place, George.

GEORGE: I jus' tole you. Jus' last night.

LENNIE: Go on, tell again.

GEORGE: Well, it's ten acres. Got a little windmill. Got a little shack on it and a chicken run. Got a kitchen orchard. Cherries, apples, peaches, 'cots and nuts. Got a few berries. There's a place for alfalfa and plenty water to flood it. There's a pig pen. . . .

LENNIE [*breaking in*]: And rabbits, George?

GEORGE: I could easy build a few hutches. And you could feed alfalfa to them rabbits.

LENNIE: Damn right I could. [*Excitedly.*] You goddamn right I could.

GEORGE [*his voice growing warmer.*] And we could have a few pigs. I'd build a smokehouse. And when we kill a pig we could smoke the hams. When the salmon run up the river we can catch a hundred of 'em. Every Sunday we'd kill a chicken or rabbit. Mebbe we'll have a cow or a goat. And the cream is so goddamn thick you got to cut it off the pan with a knife.

LENNIE [*watching him with wide eyes, softly*]: We can live off the fat of the land.

GEORGE: Sure. All kinds of vegetables in the garden and if we want a little whiskey we can sell some eggs or somethin'. And we wouldn't sleep in no bunkhouse. Nobody could can us in the middle of a job.

LENNIE [*begging*]: Tell about the house, George.

GEORGE: Sure. We'd have a little house. And a room to ourselves. And it ain't enough land so we'd have to work too hard. Mebbe six, seven hours a day only. We wouldn't have to buck no barley eleven hours a day. And when we put in a crop, why we'd be there to take that crop up. We'd know what come of our planting.

LENNIE [*eagerly*]: And rabbits. And I'd take care of them. Tell how I'd do that, George.

GEORGE: Sure. You'd go out in the alfalfa patch and you'd have a sack. You'd fill up the sack and bring it in and put it in the rabbit cages.

LENNIE: They'd nibble and they'd nibble, the way they do. I seen 'em.

GEORGE: Every six weeks or so them does would throw a litter. So we'd have plenty rabbits to eat or sell. [*Pauses for inspiration.*] And we'd keep a few pigeons to go flying round and round the windmill, like they done when I was a kid. [*Seems entranced.*] And it'd be our own. And nobody could can us. If we don't like a guy we can say: "Get to hell out," and by God he's got to do it. And if a friend come along, why, we'd have an extra bunk. Know what we'd say? We'd say, "Why don't you spen' the night?" And by God he would. We'd have a setter

dog and a couple of striped cats. [*Looks sharply at* LEN-
NIE.] But you gotta watch out them cats don't get the
little rabbits.

LENNIE [*breathing hard*]: You jus' let 'em try. I'll break their
goddamn necks. I'll smash them cats flat with a stick. I'd
smash 'em flat with a stick. That's what I'd do. [*They sit
silently for a moment.*]

CANDY [*at the sound of his voice, both* LENNIE *and*
GEORGE *jump as though caught in some secret*]: You
know where's a place like that?

GEORGE [*solemnly*]: S'pose I do, what's that to you?

CANDY: You don't need to tell me where it's at. Might be
any place.

GEORGE [*relieved*]: Sure. That's right, you couldn't find it
in a hundred years.

CANDY [*excitedly*]: How much they want for a place like
that?

GEORGE [*grudgingly*]: Well, I could get it for six hundred
bucks. The ole people that owns it is flat bust. And the ole
lady needs medicine. Say, what's it to you? You got nothing to do with us!

CANDY [*softly*]: I ain't much good with only one hand. I lost
my hand right here on the ranch. That's why they didn't
can me. They give me a job swampin'. And they give me
two hundred and fifty dollars 'cause I lost my hand. An' I
got fifty more saved up right in the bank right now. That's
three hundred. And I got forty more comin' the end of
the month. Tell you what . . . [*He leans forward eagerly.*]
S'pose I went in with you guys? That's three hundred and
forty bucks I'd put in. I ain't much good, but I could cook
and tend the chickens and hoe the garden some. How'd
that be?

GEORGE [*his eyes half closed, uncertainly*]: I got to think
about that. We was always goin' to do it by ourselves. Me
an' Lennie. I never thought of nobody else.

CANDY: I'd make a will. Leave my share to you guys in case I kicked off. I ain't got no relations nor nothing. You fellas got any money? Maybe we could go there right now.

GEORGE [*disgustedly*]: We got ten bucks between us. [*He thinks.*] Say, look. If me and Lennie work a month and don't spend nothing at all, we'll have a hundred bucks. That would be four forty. I bet we could swing her for that. Then you and Lennie could go get her started and I'd get a job and make up the rest. You could sell eggs and stuff like that. [*They look at each other in amazement. Reverently.*] Jesus Christ, I bet we could swing her. [*His voice is full of wonder.*] I bet we could swing 'er.

CANDY [*scratches the stump of his wrist nervously*]: I got hurt four years ago. They'll can me pretty soon. Jest as soon as I can't swamp out no bunkhouses they'll put me on the county. Maybe if I give you guys my money, you'll let me hoe in the garden, even when I ain't no good at it. And I'll wash dishes and little chicken stuff like that. But hell, I'll be on our own place. I'll be let to work on our own place. [*Miserably.*] You seen what they done to my dog. They says he wasn't no good to himself nor nobody else. But when I'm that way nobody'll shoot me. I wish somebody would. They won't do nothing like that. I won't have no place to go and I can't get no more jobs.

GEORGE [*stands up*]: We'll do 'er! God damn, we'll fix up that little ole place and we'll go live there. [*Wonderingly.*] S'pose they was a carnival, or a circus come to town or a ball game or any damn thing. [CANDY *nods in appreciation.*] We'd just go to her. We wouldn't ask nobody if we could. Just say we'll go to her, by God, and we would. Just milk the cow and sling some grain to the chickens and go to her.

LENNIE: And put some grass to the rabbits. I wouldn't forget to feed them. When we gonna to do it, George?

GEORGE [*decisively*]: In one month. Right squack in one month. Know what I'm gonna do? I'm goin' write to them ole people that owns the place that we'll take 'er. And Candy'll send a hundred dollars to bind her.

CANDY [*happily*]: I sure will. They got a good stove there?

GEORGE: Sure, got a nice stove. Burns coal or wood.

LENNIE: I'm gonna take my pup. I bet by Christ he likes it there. [*The window, center backstage, swings outward.* CURLEY'S WIFE *looks in. They do not see her.*]

GEORGE [*quickly*]: Now don't tell nobody about her. Jus' us three and nobody else. They'll liable to can us so we can't make no stake. We'll just go on like we was a bunch of punks. Like we was gonna buck barley the rest of our lives. And then all of a sudden, one day, bang! We get our pay and scram out of here.

CANDY: I can give you three hundred right now.

LENNIE: And not tell nobody. We won't tell nobody, George.

GEORGE: You're goddamn right we won't. [*There is a silence and then* GEORGE *speaks irritably.*] You know, seems to me I can almost smell that carnation stuff that goddamn tart dumps on herself.

CURLEY'S WIFE [*in the first part of the speech by* GEORGE *she starts to step out of sight but at the last words her face darkens with anger. At her first words everybody in the room looks around at her and remains rigid during her tirade*]: Who you callin' a tart! I come from a nice home. I was brung up by nice people. Nobody never got to me before I was married. I was straight. I tell you I was good. [*A little plaintively.*] I was. [*Angrily again.*] You know Curley. You know he wouldn't stay with me if he wasn't sure. I tell you Curley is sure. You got no right to call me a tart.

GEORGE [*sullenly*]: If you ain't a tart, what you always hangin' round guys for? You got a house an' you got a man. We don't want no trouble from you.

CURLEY'S WIFE [*pleadingly*]: Sure I got a man. He ain't never home. I got nobody to talk to. I got nobody to be with. Think I can just sit home and do nothin' but cook for Curley? I want to see somebody. Just see 'em an' talk to 'em. There ain't no women. I can't walk to town. And Curley don't take me to no dances now. I tell you I jus' want to talk to somebody.

GEORGE [*boldly*]: If you're just friendly what you givin' out the eye for an' floppin' your can around?

CURLEY'S WIFE [*sadly*]: I just wanta be nice.

The sound of approaching voices. "You don't have to get mad about it, do you?" . . . "I ain't mad, but I just don't want no more questions, that's all. I just don't want no more questions."

GEORGE: Get goin'. We don't want no trouble.

CURLEY'S WIFE *looks from the window and closes it silently and disappears. Enter* SLIM, *followed by* CURLEY, CARLSON *and* WHIT. SLIM'S *hands are black with tar.* CURLEY *hangs close to his elbow.*

CURLEY [*explaining*]: Well, I didn't mean nothing, Slim. I jus' ast you.

SLIM: Well, you been askin' too often. I'm gettin' goddamn sick of it. If you can't look after your own wife, what you expect me to do about it? You lay off of me.

CURLEY: I'm jus' tryin' to tell you I didn't mean nothing. I just thought you might of saw her.

CARLSON: Why don't you tell her to stay the hell home where she belongs? You let her hang around the bunkhouses and pretty soon you're goin' have somethin' on your hands.

CURLEY [*whirls on* CARLSON]: You keep out of this 'less you want ta step outside.

CARLSON [*laughing*]: Why you goddamn punk. You tried to throw a scare into Slim and you couldn't make it stick. Slim threwed a scare into you. You're yellow as a frog's belly. I don't care if you're the best boxer in the country, you come for me and I'll kick your goddamn head off.

WHIT [*joining in the attack*]: Glove full of vaseline!

CURLEY [*glares at him, then suddenly sniffs the air, like a hound*]: By God, she's been in *here*: I can smell—By God, she's been in here. [*To* GEORGE.] You was here. The other guys was outside. Now, God damn you—you talk.

GEORGE [*looks worried. He seems to make up his mind to face an inevitable situation. Stands up. Slowly takes off his coat, and folds it almost daintily. Speaks in an unemotional monotone*]: Somebody got to beat the hell outa you. I guess I'm elected. [LENNIE *has been watching, fascinated. He gives his high, nervous chuckle.*]

CURLEY [*whirls on him*]: What the hell you laughin' at?

LENNIE [*blankly*]: Huh?

CURLEY [*exploding with rage*]: Come on, you big bastard. Get up on your feet. No big son-of-a-bitch is gonna laugh at me. I'll show you who's yellow.

LENNIE *looks helplessly at* GEORGE. *Gets up and tries to retreat upstage.* CURLEY *follows slashing at him. The others mass themselves in front of the two contestants.* "That ain't no way, Curley—he ain't done nothing to you." ... "Lay off him, will you, Curley. He ain't no fighter." ... "Sock him back, big guy! Don't be afraid of him!" ... "Give him a chance, Curley. Give him a chance."

LENNIE [*crying with terror*]: George, make him leave me alone, George.

GEORGE: Get him, Lennie. Get him! [*There is a sharp cry.*

The gathering of men opens and CURLEY *is flopping about, his hand lost in* LENNIE'S *hand.*] Let go of him, Lennie. Let go! [*"He's got his hand!"* . . . *"Look at that, will you?"* . . . *"Jesus, what a guy!"* LENNIE *watches in terror the flopping man he holds.* LENNIE'S *face is covered with blood.* GEORGE *slaps* LENNIE *in the face again and again.* CURLEY *is weak and shrunken.*] Let go his hand, Lennie. Slim, come help me, while this guy's got any hand left. [*Suddenly* LENNIE *lets go. He cowers away from* GEORGE.]

LENNIE: You told me to, George. I heard you tell me to. [CURLEY *has dropped to the floor.* SLIM *and* CARLSON *bend over him and look at his hand.* SLIM *looks over at* LENNIE *with horror.*]

SLIM: We got to get him to a doctor. It looks to me like every bone in his hand is busted.

LENNIE [*crying*]: I didn't wanta. I didn't wanta hurt 'im.

SLIM: Carlson, you get the Candy wagon out. He'll have to go into Soledad and get his hand fixed up. [*Turns to the whimpering* LENNIE.] It ain't your fault. This punk had it comin' to him. But Jesus—he ain't hardly got no hand left.

GEORGE [*moving near*]: Slim, will we git canned now? Will Curley's ole man can us now?

SLIM: I don't know. [*Kneels down beside* CURLEY.] You got your sense enough to listen? [CURLEY *nods.*] Well, then you listen. I think you got your hand caught in a machine. If you don't tell nobody what happened, we won't. But you jest tell and try to get this guy canned and we'll tell everybody. And then will you get the laugh! [*Helps* CURLEY *to his feet.*] Come on now. Carlson's goin' to take you in to a doctor. [*Starts for the door, turns back to* LENNIE.] Le's see your hands. [LENNIE *sticks out both hands.*] Christ Almighty!

GEORGE: Lennie was just scairt. He didn't know what to

do. I tole you nobody ought never to fight him. No, I guess
it was Candy I tole.

CANDY [*solemnly*]: That's just what you done. Right this
morning when Curley first lit into him. You says he better not fool with Lennie if he knows what's good for him.
[*They all leave the stage except* GEORGE *and* LENNIE
and CANDY.]

GEORGE [*to* LENNIE, *very gently*]: It ain't your fault. You
don't need to be scairt no more. You done jus' what I tole
you to. Maybe you better go in the washroom and clean
up your face. You look like hell.

LENNIE: I didn't want no trouble.

GEORGE: Come on—I'll go with you.

LENNIE: George?

GEORGE: What you want?

LENNIE: Can I still tend the rabbits, George?

*They exeunt together, side by side, through the door of
the bunkhouse.*

CURTAIN

ACT TWO: SCENE II

Ten o'clock Saturday evening.

The room of the stable buck, a lean-to off the barn. There is a plank door up stage center; a small square window center right. On one side of the door a leather working bench with tools racked behind it, and on the other racks with broken and partly mended harnesses, collars, hames, traces, etc. At the left upstage CROOKS' *bunk. Over it two shelves. On one a great number of medicines in cans and bottles. And on the other a number of tattered books and a big alarm clock. In the corner right upstage a single-barreled shotgun and on the floor beside it a pair of rubber boots. A large pair of gold spectacles hangs on a nail over* CROOKS' *bunk.*

The entrance leads into the barn proper. From that direction and during the whole scene come the sounds of horses eating, stamping, jingling their halter chains and now and then whinnying.

Two empty nail kegs are in the room to be used as seats. Single unshaded small-candle-power carbon light hanging from its own cord.

As the curtain rises, we see CROOKS *sitting on his bunk rubbing his back with liniment. He reaches up under his shirt to do this. His face is lined with pain. As he rubs he flexes his muscles and shivers a little.*

LENNIE *appears in the open doorway, nearly filling the opening. Then* CROOKS, *sensing his presence, raises his eyes, stiffens and scowls.*

LENNIE *smiles in an attempt to make friends.*

CROOKS [*sharply*]: You got no right to come in my room. This here's my room. Nobody got any right in here but me.

LENNIE [*fawning*]: I ain't doin' nothing. Just come in the barn to look at my pup, and I seen your light.

CROOKS: Well, I got a right to have a light. You go on and get out of my room. I ain't wanted in the bunkhouse and you ain't wanted in my room.

LENNIE [*ingenuously*]: Why ain't you wanted?

CROOKS [*furiously*]: 'Cause I'm black. They play cards in there. But I can't play because I'm black. They say I stink. Well, I tell you all of you stink to me.

LENNIE [*helplessly*]: Everybody went into town. Slim and George and everybody. George says I got to stay here and not get into no trouble. I seen your light.

CROOKS: Well, what do you want?

LENNIE: Nothing . . . I seen your light. I thought I could jus' come in and set.

CROOKS [*stares at* LENNIE *for a moment, takes down his spectacles and adjusts them over his ears; says in a complaining tone*]: I don't know what you're doin' in the barn anyway. You ain't no skinner. There's no call for a bucker to come into the barn at all. You've got nothing to do with the horses and mules.

LENNIE [*patiently*]: The pup. I come to see my pup.

CROOKS: Well, God damn it, go and see your pup then. Don't go no place where you ain't wanted.

LENNIE [*advances a step into the room, remembers and backs to the door again*]: I looked at him a little. Slim says I ain't to pet him very much.

CROOKS [*the anger gradually going out of his voice*]: Well, you been taking him out of the nest all the time. I wonder the ole lady don't move him some place else.

LENNIE [*moving into the room*]: Oh, she don't care. She lets me.

CROOKS [*scowls and then gives up*]: Come on in and set awhile. Long as you won't get out and leave me alone, you might as well set down. [*A little more friendly.*] All the boys gone into town, huh?

LENNIE: All but old Candy. He jus' sets in the bunkhouse sharpening his pencils. And sharpening and figurin'.

CROOKS [*adjusting his glasses*]: Figurin'? What's Candy figurin' about?

LENNIE: 'Bout the land. 'Bout the little place.

CROOKS: You're nuts. You're crazy as a wedge. What land you talkin' about?

LENNIE: The land we're goin' ta get. And a little house and pigeons.

CROOKS: Just nuts. I don't blame the guy you're traveling with for keeping you out of sight.

LENNIE [*quietly*]: It ain't no lie. We're gonna do it. Gonna get a little place and live on the fat of the land.

CROOKS [*settling himself comfortably on his bunk*]: Set down. Set down on that nail keg.

LENNIE [*hunches over on the little barrel*]: You think it's a lie. But it ain't no lie. Ever' word's the truth. You can ask George.

CROOKS [*puts his dark chin on his palm*]: You travel round with George, don't you?

LENNIE [*proudly*]: Sure, me and him goes ever' place together.

CROOKS [*after a pause, quietly*]: Sometimes he talks and you don't know what the hell he's talkin' about. Ain't that so? [*Leans forward.*] Ain't that so?

LENNIE: Yeah. Sometimes.

CROOKS: Just talks on. And you don't know what the hell it's all about.

LENNIE: How long you think it'll be before them pups will be old enough to pet?

CROOKS [*laughs again*]: A guy can talk to you and be sure you won't go blabbin'. A couple of weeks and them pups will be all right. [*Musing.*] George knows what he's about. Just talks and you don't understand nothing. [*Mood gradually changes to excitement.*] Well, this is just a nigger talkin' and a busted-back nigger. It don't mean nothing, see. You couldn't remember it anyway. I seen it over and over—a guy talking to another guy and it don't make no difference if he don't hear or understand. The thing is they're talkin'. [*He pounds his knee with his hand.*] George can tell you screwy things and it don't matter. It's just the talkin'. It's just bein' with another guy, that's all. [*His voice becomes soft and malicious.*] S'pose George don't come back no more? S'pose he took a powder and just ain't comin' back. What you do then?

LENNIE [*trying to follow* CROOKS]: What? What?

CROOKS: I said s'pose George went into town tonight and you never heard of him no more. [*Presses forward.*] Just s'pose that.

LENNIE [*sharply*]: He won't do it. George wouldn't do nothing like that. I been with George a long time. He'll come back tonight. . . . [*Doubt creeps into his voice.*] Don't you think he will?

CROOKS [*delighted with his torture*]: Nobody can tell what a guy will do. Let's say he wants to come back and can't. S'pose he gets killed or hurt so he can't come back.

LENNIE [*in terrible apprehension*]: I don't know. Say, what you doin' anyway? It ain't true. George ain't got hurt.

CROOKS [*cruelly*]: Want me to tell you what'll happen?

They'll take you to the booby hatch. They'll tie you up with a collar like a dog. Then you'll be jus' like me. Livin' in a kennel.

LENNIE [*furious, walks over towards* CROOKS]: Who hurt George?

CROOKS [*recoiling from him with fright*]: I was just supposin'. George ain't hurt. He's all right. He'll be back all right.

LENNIE [*standing over him*]: What you supposin' for? Ain't nobody goin' to s'pose any hurt to George.

CROOKS [*trying to calm him*]: Now set down. George ain't hurt. Go on now, set down.

LENNIE [*growling*]: Ain't nobody gonna talk no hurt to George.

CROOKS [*very gently*]: Maybe you can see now. You got George. You know he's comin' back. S'pose you didn't have nobody. S'pose you couldn't go in the bunkhouse and play rummy, 'cause you was black. How would you like that? S'pose you had to set out here and read books. Sure, you could play horseshoes until it got dark, but then you got to read books. Books ain't no good. A guy needs somebody . . . to be near him. [*His tone whines.*] A guy goes nuts if he ain't got nobody. Don't make no difference who it is as long as he's with you. I tell you a guy gets too lonely, he gets sick.

LENNIE [*reassuring himself*]: George gonna come back. Maybe George come back already. Maybe I better go see.

CROOKS [*more gently*]: I didn't mean to scare you. He'll come back. I was talkin' about myself.

LENNIE [*miserably*]: George won't go away and leave me. I know George won't do that.

CROOKS [*continuing dreamily*]: I remember when I was a little kid on my ole man's chicken ranch. Had two brothers. They was always near me, always there. Used to sleep right in the same room. Right in the same bed, all three. Had a strawberry patch. Had an alfalfa patch. Used to turn the chickens out in the alfalfa on a sunny morning. Me and my brothers would set on the fence and watch 'em—white chickens they was.

LENNIE [*interested*]: George says we're gonna have alfalfa.

CROOKS: You're nuts.

LENNIE: We are too gonna get it. You ask George.

CROOKS [*scornfully*]: You're nuts. I seen hundreds of men come by on the road and on the ranches, bindles on their back and that same damn thing in their head. Hundreds of 'em. They come and they quit and they go on. And every damn one of 'em is got a little piece of land in his head. And never a goddamn one of 'em gets it. Jus' like heaven. Everybody wants a little piece of land. Nobody never gets to heaven. And nobody gets no land.

LENNIE: We are too.

CROOKS: It's jest in your head. Guys all the time talkin' about it, but it's jest in your head. [*The horses move restlessly. One of them whinnies.*] I guess somebody's out there. Maybe Slim. [*Pulls himself painfully upright and moves toward the door. Calls.*] That you, Slim?

CANDY [*from outside*]: Slim went in town. Say, you seen Lennie?

CROOKS: You mean the big guy?

CANDY: Yes. Seen him around any place?

CROOKS [*goes back to his bunk and sits down, says shortly*]: He's in here.

CANDY [*stands in the doorway, scratching his wrist. Makes no attempt to enter*]: Look, Lennie, I been figuring something out. About the place.

CROOKS [*irritably*]: You can come in if you want.

CANDY [*embarrassed*]: I don't know. Course if you want me to.

CROOKS: Oh, come on in. Everybody's comin' in. You might just as well. Gettin' to be a goddamn race track. [*He tries to conceal his pleasure.*]

CANDY [*still embarrassed*]: You've got a nice cozy little place in here. Must be nice to have a room to yourself this way.

CROOKS: Sure. And a manure pile under the window. All to myself. It's swell.

LENNIE [*breaking in*]: You said about the place.

CANDY: You know, I been here a long time. An' Crooks been here a long time. This is the first time I ever been in his room.

CROOKS [*darkly*]: Guys don't come in a colored man's room. Nobody been here but Slim.

LENNIE [*insistently*]: The place. You said about the place.

CANDY: Yeah. I got it all figured out. We can make some real money on them rabbits if we go about it right.

LENNIE: But I get to tend 'em. George says I get to tend 'em. He promised.

CROOKS [*brutally*]: You guys is just kiddin' yourselves. You'll talk about it a hell of a lot, but you won't get no land. You'll be a swamper here until they take you out in a box. Hell, I seen too many guys.

CANDY [*angrily*]: We're gonna do it. George says we are. We got the money right now.

CROOKS: Yeah. And where is George now? In town in a whorehouse. That's where your money's goin'. I tell you I seen it happen too many times.

CANDY: George ain't got the money in town. The money's in the bank. Me and Lennie and George. We gonna have a room to ourselves. We gonna have a dog and chickens. We gonna have green corn and maybe a cow.

CROOKS [*impressed*]: You say you got the money?

CANDY: We got most of it. Just a little bit more to get. Have it all in one month. George's got the land all picked out too.

CROOKS [*exploring his spine with his hands*]: I've never seen a guy really do it. I seen guys nearly crazy with loneliness for land, but every time a whorehouse or a blackjack game took it away from 'em. [*Hesitates and then speaks timidly.*] If you guys would want a hand to work for noth in'—just his keep, why I'd come and lend a hand. I ain't so crippled I can't work like a son-of-a-bitch if I wanted to.

GEORGE [*strolls through the door, hands in pockets, leans against the wall, speaks in a half-satiric, rather gentle voice*]: You couldn't go to bed like I told you, could you, Lennie? Hell, no—you got to get out in society an' flap your mouth. Holdin' a convention out here.

LENNIE [*defending himself*]: You was gone. There wasn't nobody in the bunkhouse. I ain't done no bad things, George.

GEORGE [*still casually*]: Only time I get any peace is when you're asleep. If you ever get walkin' in your sleep I'll chop off your head like a chicken. [*Chops with his hand.*]

CROOKS [*coming to* LENNIE'S *defense*]: We was jus' settin' here talkin'. Ain't no harm in that.

GEORGE: Yeah. I heard you. [*A weariness has settled on him.*] Got to be here ever' minute, I guess. Got to watch ya. [*To* CROOKS.] It ain't nothing against you, Crooks. We just wasn't gonna tell nobody.

CANDY [*tries to change subject*]: Didn't you have no fun in town?

GEORGE: Oh! I set in a chair and Susy was crackin' jokes an' the guys was startin' to raise a little puny hell. Christ Almighty—I never been this way before. I'm jus' gonna set out a dime and a nickel for a shot an' I think what a hell of a lot of bulk carrot seed you can get for fifteen cents.

CANDY: Not in them damn little envelopes—but bulk seed—you sure can.

GEORGE: So purty soon I come back. I can't think of nothing else. Them guys slingin' money around got me jumpy.

CANDY: Guy got to have *some* fun. I was to a parlor house in Bakersfield once. God Almighty, what a place. Went upstairs on a red carpet. They was big pitchers on the wall. We set in big sof' chairs. They was cigarettes on the table—an' they was *free*. Purty soon a Jap come in with drinks on a tray an' them *drinks* was free. Take all you want. [*In a reverie.*] Purty soon the girls come in an' they was jus' as polite an' nice an' quiet an' purty. Didn't seem like hookers. Made ya kinda scared to ask 'em. . . . That was a long time ago.

GEORGE: Yeah? An' what'd them sof' chairs set you back?

CANDY: Fifteen bucks.

GEORGE [*scornfully*]: So ya got a cigarette an' a whiskey an' a look at a purty dress an' it cost ya twelve and a half bucks extra. You shot a week's pay to walk on that red carpet.

CANDY [*still entranced with his memory*]: A week's pay? Sure. But I worked weeks all my life. I can't remember none of them weeks. But . . . that was nearly twenty years ago. And I can remember that. Girl I went with was named Arline. Had on a pink silk dress.

GEORGE [*turns suddenly and looks out the door into the dark barn, speaks savagely*]: I s'pose ya lookin' for Curley? [CURLEY'S WIFE *appears in the door.*] Well, Curley ain't here.

CURLEY'S WIFE [*determined now*]: I know Curley ain't here. I wanted to ast Crooks somepin'. I didn't know you guys was here.

CANDY: Didn't George tell you before—we don't want nothing to do with you. You know damn well Curley ain't here.

CURLEY'S WIFE: I know where Curley went. Got his arm in a sling an' he went anyhow. I tell ya I come out to ast Crooks somepin'.

CROOKS [*apprehensively*]: Maybe you better go along to

your own house. You hadn't ought to come near a colored
man's room. I don't want no trouble. You don't want to
ask me nothing.

CANDY [*rubbing his wrist stump*]: You got a husband. You
got no call to come foolin' around with other guys, causin'
trouble.

CURLEY'S WIFE [*suddenly angry*]: I try to be nice an' polite
to you lousy bindle bums—but you're too good. I tell ya I
could of went with shows. An'—an' a guy wanted to put
me in pitchers right in Hollywood. [*Looks about to see
how she is impressing them. Their eyes are hard.*] I come
out here to ast somebody somepin' an'—

CANDY [*stands up suddenly and knocks his nail keg over
backward, speaks angrily*]: I had enough. You ain't wanted
here. We tole you, you ain't. Callin' us bindle stiffs. You
got floozy idears what us guys amounts to. You ain't got
sense enough to see us guys ain't bindle stiffs. S'pose you
could get us *canned*—s'pose you *could*. You think we'd
hit the highway an' look for another two-bit job. You
don't know we got our own ranch to go to an' our own
house an' fruit trees. An' we got friends. That's what we
got. Maybe they was a time when we didn't have nothing,
but that ain't so no more.

CURLEY'S WIFE: You damn ol' goat. If you had two bits,
you'd be in Soledad gettin' a drink an' suckin' the bottom
of the glass.

GEORGE: Maybe she could ask Crooks what she come to
ask an' then get the hell home. I don't think she come to
ask nothing.

CURLEY'S WIFE: What happened to Curley's hand?
[CROOKS *laughs.* GEORGE *tries to shut him up.*] So it
wasn't no machine. Curley didn't act like he was tellin' the
truth. Come on, Crooks—what happened?

CROOKS: I wasn't there. I didn't see it.

CURLEY'S WIFE [*eagerly*]: What happened? I won't let on

to Curley. He says he caught his han' in a gear. [CROOKS *is silent.*] Who done it?

GEORGE: Didn't nobody do it.

CURLEY'S WIFE [*turns slowly to* GEORGE]: So *you* done it. Well, he had it comin'.

GEORGE: I didn't have no fuss with Curley.

CURLEY'S WIFE [*steps near him, smiling*]: Maybe now you ain't scared of him no more. Maybe you'll talk to me sometimes now. Ever'body was scared of him.

GEORGE [*speaks rather kindly*]: Look! I didn't sock Curley. If he had trouble, it ain't none of our affair. Ask Curley about it. Now listen. I'm gonna try to tell ya. We tole you to get the hell out and it don't do no good. So I'm gonna tell you another way. Us guys got somepin' we're gonna do. If you stick around you'll gum up the works. It ain't your fault. If a guy steps on a round pebble an' falls down an' breaks his neck, it ain't the pebble's fault, but the guy wouldn't of did it if the pebble wasn't there.

CURLEY'S WIFE [*puzzled*]: What you talkin' about pebbles? If you didn't sock Curley, who did? [*She looks at the others, then steps quickly over to* LENNIE.] Where'd you get them bruises on your face?

GEORGE: I tell you he got his hand caught in a machine.

LENNIE [*looks anxiously at* GEORGE, *speaks miserably*]: He caught his han' in a machine.

GEORGE: So now get out of here.

CURLEY'S WIFE [*goes close to* LENNIE, *speaks softly and there is a note of affection in her voice*]: So . . . it was you. Well . . . maybe you're dumb like they say . . . an' maybe . . . you're the only guy on the ranch with guts. [*She puts her hand on* LENNIE'S *shoulder. He looks up in her face and a smile grows on his face. She strokes his shoulder.*] You're a nice fella.

GEORGE [*suddenly leaps at her ferociously, grabs her shoulder and whirls her around*]: Listen . . . you! I tried to give you a break. Don't you walk into nothing! We ain't gonna let you mess up what we're gonna do. You let this guy alone an' get the hell out of here.

CURLEY'S WIFE [*defiant but slightly frightened*]: You ain't tellin' me what to do. [*The* BOSS *appears in the door, stands legs spread, thumbs hooked over his belt.*] I got a right to talk to anybody I want to.

GEORGE: Why, you—[GEORGE, *furious, steps close—his hand is raised to strike her. She cowers a little.* GEORGE *stiffens, seeing* BOSS, *frozen in position. The others see* BOSS *too. Girl retreats slowly.* GEORGE'S *hand drops slowly to his side—he takes two slow backward steps. Hold the scene for a moment.*]

CURTAIN

ACT THREE

ACT THREE: SCENE I

Mid-afternoon Sunday.

One end of a great barn. Backstage the hay slopes up sharply against the wall. High in the upstage wall is a large hay window. On each side are seen the hay racks, behind which are the stalls with the horses in them. Throughout this scene the horses can be heard in their stalls, rattling their halter chains and chewing at the hay.

The entrance is downstage right.

The boards of the barn are not close together. Streaks of afternoon sun come between the boards, made visible by dust in the air. From outside comes the clang of horseshoes on the playing peg, shouts of men encouraging or jeering.

In the barn there is a feeling of quiet and humming and lazy warmth. Curtain rises on LENNIE *sitting in the hay, looking down at a little dead puppy in front of him. He puts out his big hand and strokes it clear from one end to the other.*

LENNIE [*softly*]: Why do you got to get killed? You ain't so little as mice. I didn' bounce you hard. [*Bends the pup's head up and looks in its face.*] Now maybe George ain't gonna let me tend no rabbits if he finds out you got killed. [*He scoops a little hollow and lays the puppy in it out of sight and covers it over with hay. He stares at the mound he has made.*] This ain't no bad thing like I got to hide in the brush. I'll tell George I found it dead. [*He unburies the pup and inspects it. Twists its ears and works his fingers in its fur. Sorrowfully.*] But he'll know. George always knows. He'll say: "You done it. Don't try to put nothin' over on me." And he'll say: "Now just for that you don't get to tend no—you-know-whats." [*His anger rises. Addresses the pup.*] God damn you. Why do you got to get killed? You ain't so little as mice. [*Picks up the pup and hurls it from him and turns his back on it. He sits bent over his knees moaning to himself.*] Now he won't let me. . . . Now he won't let me. [*Outside there is a clang of horseshoes on the iron stake and a little chorus of cries.* LENNIE *gets up and brings the pup back and lays it in the hay and sits down. He mourns.*] You wasn't big enough. They tole me and tole me you wasn't. I didn't know you'd get killed so easy. Maybe George won't care. This here goddamn little son-of-a-bitch wasn't nothin' to George.

CANDY [*voice from behind the stalls*]: Lennie, where you at? [LENNIE *frantically buries the pup under the hay.* CANDY *enters excitedly.*] Thought I'd find ya here. Say . . . I been talkin' to Slim. It's okay. We ain't gonna get the can. Slim been talkin' to the boss. Slim tol' the boss you guys is good buckers. The boss got to move that grain. 'Member what hell the boss give us las' night? He tol' Slim he got his eye on you an' George. But you ain't gonna get the can. Oh! an' say. The boss give Curley's wife hell, too. Tole her never to go near the men no more. Give her worse hell than you an' George. [*For the first time notices* LENNIE'S *dejection.*] Ain't you glad?

LENNIE: Sure.

CANDY: You ain't sick?

LENNIE: Uh-uh!

CANDY: I got to go tell George. See you later. [*Exits.*]

> LENNIE, *alone, uncovers the pup. Lies down in the hay*
> *and sinks deep in it. Puts the pup on his arm and strokes*
> *it.* CURLEY'S WIFE *enters secretly. A little mound of hay*
> *conceals* LENNIE *from her. In her hand she carries a small*
> *suitcase, very cheap. She crosses the barn and buries the*
> *case in the hay. Stands up and looks to see whether it can*
> *be seen.* LENNIE *watching her quietly tries to cover the*
> *pup with hay. She sees the movement.*

CURLEY'S WIFE: What—what you doin' here?

LENNIE [*sullenly*]: Jus' settin' here.

CURLEY'S WIFE: You seen what I done.

LENNIE: Yeah! You brang a valise.

CURLEY'S WIFE [*comes near to him*]: You won't tell—will you?

LENNIE [*still sullen*]: I ain't gonna have nothing to do with you. George tole me. I ain't to talk to you or nothing. [*Covers the pup a little more.*]

CURLEY'S WIFE: George give you all your orders?

LENNIE: Not talk nor nothing.

CURLEY'S WIFE: You won't tell about that suitcase? I ain't gonna stay here no more. Tonight I'm gonna get out. Come here an' get my stuff an' get out. I ain't gonna be run over no more. I'm gonna go in pitchers. [*Sees* LENNIE'S *hand stroking the pup under the hay.*] What you got there?

LENNIE: Nuthing. I ain't gonna talk to you. George says I ain't.

CURLEY'S WIFE: Listen: The guys got a horseshoe tenement out there. It's on'y four o'clock. Them guys ain't gonna leave that tenement. They got money bet. You don't need to be scared to talk to me.

LENNIE [*weakening a little*]: I ain't supposed to.

CURLEY'S WIFE [*watching his buried hand*]: What you got under there?

LENNIE [*his woe comes back to him*]: Jus' my pup. Jus' my little ol' pup. [*Sweeps the hay aside.*]

CURLEY'S WIFE: Why! He's dead.

LENNIE [*explaining sadly*]: He was so little. I was jus' playin' with him—an' he made like he's gonna bite me—an' I made like I'm gonna smack him—an'—I done it. An' then he was dead.

CURLEY'S WIFE [*consolingly*]: Don't you worry none. He was just a mutt. The whole country is full of mutts.

LENNIE: It ain't that so much. George gonna be mad. Maybe he won't let me—what he said I could tend.

CURLEY'S WIFE [*sits down in the hay beside him, speaks soothingly*]: Don't you worry. Them guys got money bet on that horseshoe tenement. They ain't gonna leave it. And tomorra I'll be gone. I ain't gonna let them run over me.

In the following scene it is apparent that neither is listening to the other and yet as it goes on, as a happy tone increases, it can be seen that they are growing closer together.

LENNIE: We gonna have a little place an' raspberry bushes.

CURLEY'S WIFE: I ain't meant to live like this. I come from Salinas. Well, a show come through an' I talked to a guy that was in it. He says I could go with the show. My ol' lady wouldn' let me, 'cause I was on'y fifteen. I wouldn't be no place like this if I had went with that show, you bet.

LENNIE: Gonna take a sack an' fill it up with alfalfa an'—

CURLEY'S WIFE [*hurrying on*]: 'Nother time I met a guy an'

he was in pitchers. Went out to the Riverside Dance Palace with him. He said he was gonna put me in pitchers. Says I was a natural. Soon's he got back to Hollywood he was gonna write me about it. [*Looks impressively at* LENNIE.] I never got that letter. I think my ol' lady stole it. Well, I wasn't gonna stay no place where they stole your letters. So I married Curley. Met *him* out to the Riverside Dance Palace too.

LENNIE: I hope George ain't gonna be mad about this pup.

CURLEY'S WIFE: I ain't tol' this to nobody before. Maybe I oughtn' to. I don't like Curley. He ain't a nice fella. I might a stayed with him but last night him an' his ol' man both lit into me. I don't have to stay here. [*Moves closer and speaks confidentially.*] Don't tell nobody till I get clear away. I'll go in the night an' thumb a ride to Hollywood.

LENNIE: We gonna get out a here purty soon. This ain't no nice place.

CURLEY'S WIFE [*ecstatically*]: Gonna get in the movies an' have nice clothes—all them nice clothes like they wear. An' I'll set in them big hotels and they'll take pitchers of me. When they have them openings I'll go an' talk in the radio . . . an' it won't cost me nothing 'cause I'm in the pitcher. [*Puts her hand on* LENNIE'S *arm for a moment.*] All them nice clothes like they wear . . . because this guy says I'm a natural.

LENNIE: We gonna go way . . . far away from here.

CURLEY'S WIFE: 'Course, when I run away from Curley, my ol' lady won't never speak to me no more. She'll think I ain't decent. That's what she'll say. [*Defiantly.*] Well, we really ain't decent, no matter how much my ol' lady tries to hide it, My ol' man was a drunk. They put him away. There! Now I told.

LENNIE: George an' me was to the Sacramento Fair. One time I fell in the river an' George pulled me out an' saved me, an' then we went to the Fair. They got all kinds of stuff there. We seen long-hair rabbits.

CURLEY'S WIFE: My ol' man was a sign-painter when he worked. He used to get drunk an' paint crazy pitchers an' waste paint. One night when I was a little kid, him an' my ol' lady had an awful fight. They was always fightin'. In the middle of the night he come into my room, and he says, "I can't stand this no more. Let's you an' me go away." I guess he was drunk. [*Her voice takes on a curious wondering tenderness.*] I remember in the night—walkin' down the road, and the trees was black. I was pretty sleepy. He picked me up, an' he carried me on his back. He says, "We gonna live together. We gonna live together because you're my own little girl, an' not no stranger. No arguin' and fightin'," he says, "because you're my little daughter." [*Her voice becomes soft.*] He says, "Why you'll bake little cakes for me, an' I'll paint pretty pitchers all over the wall." [*Sadly.*] In the morning they caught us . . . an' they put him away. [*Pause.*] I wish we'd a' went.

LENNIE: Maybe if I took this here pup an' throwed him away George wouldn't never know.

CURLEY'S WIFE: They locked him up for a drunk, and in a little while he died.

LENNIE: Then maybe I could tend the rabbits without no trouble.

CURLEY'S WIFE: Don't you think of nothing but rabbits? [*Sound of horseshoe on metal.*] Somebody made a ringer.

LENNIE [*patiently*]: We gonna have a house and a garden, an' a place for alfalfa. And I take a sack and get it all full of alfalfa, and then I take it to the rabbits.

CURLEY'S WIFE: What makes you so nuts about rabbits?

LENNIE [*moves close to her*]: I like to pet nice things. Once at a fair I seen some of them long-hair rabbits. And they was nice, you bet. [*Despairingly.*] I'd even pet mice, but not when I could get nothin' better.

CURLEY'S WIFE [*giggles*]: I think you're nuts.

LENNIE [*earnestly*]: No, I ain't. George says I ain't. I like to pet nice things with my fingers. Soft things.

CURLEY'S WIFE: Well, who don't? Everybody likes that. I like to feel silk and velvet. You like to feel velvet?

LENNIE [*chuckling with pleasure*]: You bet, by God. And I had some too. A lady give me some. And that lady was—my Aunt Clara. She give it right to me.... [*Measuring with his hands.*] 'Bout this big a piece. I wisht I had that velvet right now. [*He frowns.*] I lost it. I ain't seen it for a long time.

CURLEY'S WIFE [*laughing*]: You're nuts. But you're a kinda nice fella. Jus' like a big baby. A person can see kinda what you mean. When I'm doin' my hair sometimes I jus' set there and stroke it, because it's so soft. [*Runs her fingers over the top of her head.*] Some people got kinda coarse hair. You take Curley, his hair's just like wire. But mine is soft and fine. Here, feel. Right here. [*Takes LENNIE's hand and puts it on her head.*] Feel there and see how soft it is. [LENNIE'S *fingers fall to stroking her hair.*] Don't you muss it up.

LENNIE: Oh, that's nice. [*Strokes harder.*] Oh, that's nice.

CURLEY'S WIFE: Look out now, you'll muss it. [*Angrily.*] You stop it now, you'll mess it all up. [*She jerks her head sideways and* Lennie's *fingers close on her hair and hang on. In a panic.*] Let go. [*She screams.*] You let go. [*She screams again. His other hand closes over her mouth and nose.*]

LENNIE [*begging*]: Oh, please don't do that. George'll be mad. [*She struggles violently to be free. A soft screaming comes from under* LENNIE'S *hand. Crying with fright.*] Oh, please don't do none of that. George gonna say I done a bad thing. [*He raises his hand from her mouth and a hoarse cry escapes. Angrily.*] Now don't. I don't want you to yell. You gonna get me in trouble just like George says you will. Now don't you do that. [*She struggles more.*] Don't you go yellin'. [*He shakes her violently. Her neck snaps sideways and she lies still. Looks down at her and cautiously removes his hand from over her mouth.*] I don't wanta hurt you. But George will be mad if you yell. [*When she doesn't answer he bends closely over her. He lifts her arm and lets it drop. For a moment he seems bewildered.*] I done a bad thing. I done another bad thing. [*He paws up the hay until it partly covers her. The sound of the horseshoe game comes from the outside. And for the first time* LENNIE *seems conscious of it. He crouches down and listens.*] Oh, I done a real bad thing. I shouldn't a did that. George will be mad. And . . . he said . . . and hide in the brush till he comes. . . . He's gonna be mad . . . in the brush till he comes. That's what he said. [*He picks up the puppy from beside the girl.*] I'll throw him away. It's bad enough like it is.

He puts the pup under his coat, creeps to the barn wall and peers out between the cracks and then he creeps around to the end of the manger and disappears. The stage is vacant except for CURLEY'S WIFE. *She lies in the hay half covered up and she looks very young and peaceful. Her rouged cheeks and red lips make her seem alive and sleeping lightly. For a moment the stage is absolutely silent. Then the horses stamp on the other side of the feeding rack. The halter chains clink and from outside men's voices come loud and clear.*

CANDY [*offstage*]: Lennie! Oh, Lennie, you in there? [*He enters.*] I been figurin' some more, Lennie. Tell you what we can do. [*Sees* CURLEY'S WIFE *and stops. Rubs his white whiskers.*] I didn't know you was here. You was tol' not to be here. [*He steps near her.*] You oughtn't to sleep out here. [*He is right beside her and looks down.*] Oh,

Jesus Christ! [*Goes to the door and calls softly.*] George, George! Come here . . . George!

GEORGE [*enters*]: What do you want?

CANDY [*points at* CURLEY'S WIFE]: Look.

GEORGE: What's the matter with her? [*Steps up beside her.*] Oh, Jesus Christ!

Kneels beside her and feels her heart and her wrist. Finally stands up slowly and stiffly. From this time on through the rest of the scene GEORGE *is wooden.*

CANDY: What done it?

GEORGE [*coldly*]: Ain't you got any idea? [CANDY *looks away.*] I should of knew. I guess way back in my head I did.

CANDY: What we gonna do now, George? What we gonna do now?

GEORGE [*answering slowly and dully*]: Guess . . . we gotta . . . tell . . . the guys. Guess we got to catch him and lock him up. We can't let him get away. Why, the poor bastard would starve. [*He tries to reassure himself.*] Maybe they'll lock him up and be nice to him.

CANDY [*excitedly*]: You know better'n that, George. You know Curley's gonna want to get him lynched. You know how Curley is.

GEORGE: Yeah. . . . Yeah . . . that's right. I know Curley. And the other guys too. [*He looks back at* CURLEY'S WIFE.]

CANDY [*pleadingly*]: You and me can get that little place can't we, George? You and me can go there and live nice, can't we? Can't we? [CANDY *drops his head and looks down at the hay to indicate that he knows.*]

GEORGE [*shakes his head slowly*]: It was somethin' me and him had. [*Softly.*] I think I knowed it from the very first. I think I knowed we'd never do her. He used to like to hear about it so much. I got fooled to thinkin' maybe we would. [CANDY *starts to speak but doesn't.*]

GEORGE [*as though repeating a lesson*]: I'll work my month and then I'll take my fifty bucks. I'll stay all night in some lousy cat-house or I'll set in a pool room until everybody goes home. An' then—I'll come back an' work another month. And then I'll have fifty bucks more.

CANDY: He's such a nice fellow. I didn't think he'd a done nothing like this.

GEORGE [*gets a grip on himself and straightens his shoulders*]: Now listen. We gotta tell the guys. I guess they've gotta bring him in. They ain't no way out. Maybe they won't hurt him. I ain't gonna let 'em hurt Lennie. [*Sharply.*] Now you listen. The guys might think I was in on it. I'm gonna go in the bunkhouse. Then in a minute you come out and yell like you just seen her. Will you do that? So the guys won't think I was in on it?

CANDY: Sure, George. Sure, I'll do that.

GEORGE: Okay. Give me a couple of minutes then. And then you yell your head off. I'm goin' now. [GEORGE *exits.*]

CANDY [*watches him go, looks helplessly back at CUR-LEY'S WIFE; his next words are in sorrow and in anger*]: You goddamn tramp. You done it, didn't you? Everybody knowed you'd mess things up. You just wasn't no good. [*His voice shakes.*] I could of hoed in the garden and washed dishes for them guys.... [*Pauses for a moment and then goes into a sing-song repeating the old words.*] If there was a circus or a baseball game ... we would o' went to her ... just said to hell with work and went to her. And they'd been a pig and chickens ... and in the winter a little fat stove. An' us jus' settin' there ... settin' there.... [*His eyes blind with tears and he goes weakly to the entrance of the barn. Tries for a moment to break a shout out of his throat before he succeeds.*] Hey, you guys! Come here! Come here!

*Outside the noise of the horseshoe game stops. The sound
of discussion and then the voices come closer: "What's
the matter?" ... "Who's that?" ... "It's Candy." ...
"Something must have happened." Enter* SLIM *and* CARL-
SON, *Young* WHIT *and* CURLEY, CROOKS *in the back,
keeping out of attention range. And last of all* GEORGE.
GEORGE *has put on his blue denim coat and buttoned it.
His black hat is pulled down low over his eyes.*

"What's the matter?" ... "What's happened?"

A gesture from CANDY.

The men stare at CURLEY'S WIFE. SLIM *goes over to
her, feels her wrist and touches her cheek with his fingers.
His hand goes under her slightly twisted neck.*

CURLEY *comes near. For a moment he seems shocked.
Looks around helplessly and suddenly he comes to life.*

CURLEY: I know who done it. That big son-of-a-bitch done
it. I know he done it. Why, everybody else was out there
playing horseshoes. [*Working himself into a fury.*] I'm
gonna get him. I'm gonna get my shotgun. Why, I'll kill
the big son-of-a-bitch myself. I'll shoot him in the guts.
Come on, you guys. [*He runs out of the barn.*]

CARLSON: I'll go get my Luger. [*He runs out too.*]

SLIM [*quietly to* GEORGE]: I guess Lennie done it all right.
Her neck's busted. Lennie could o' did that. [GEORGE
nods slowly. Half-questioning.] Maybe like that time in
Weed you was tellin' me about. [GEORGE *nods. Gently.*]
Well. I guess we got to get him. Where you think he might
o' went?

GEORGE [*struggling to get words out*]: I don't know.

SLIM: I guess we gotta get him.

GEORGE [*stepping close and speaking passionately*]:
Couldn't we maybe bring him in and lock him up? He's
nuts, Slim, he never done this to be mean.

SLIM: If we could only keep Curley in. But Curley wants

to shoot him. [*He thinks.*] And s'pose they lock him up, George, and strap him down and put him in a cage, that ain't no good.

GEORGE: I know. I know.

SLIM: I think there's only one way to get him out of it.

GEORGE: I know.

CARLSON [*enters running*]: The bastard stole my Luger. It ain't in my bag.

CURLEY [*enters carrying a shotgun in his good hand. Officiously*]: All right, you guys. The nigger's got a shotgun. You take it, Carlson.

WHIT: Only cover around here is down by the river. He might have went there.

CURLEY: Don't give him no chance. Shoot for his guts, that'll double him over.

WHIT: I ain't got a gun.

CURLEY: Go in and tell my old man. Get a gun from him. Let's go now. [*Turns suspiciously on* GEORGE.] You're comin' with us, fella!

GEORGE: Yeah. I'll come. But listen, Curley, the poor bastard's nuts. Don't shoot him, he didn't know what he was doin'.

CURLEY: Don't shoot him! He's got Carlson's Luger, ain't he?

GEORGE [*weakly*]: Maybe Carlson lost his gun.

CARLSON: I seen it this morning. It's been took.

SLIM [*looking down at* CURLEY'S WIFE]: Curley, maybe you better stay here with your wife. [*The light is fading into evening.* CURLEY *hesitates. Seems almost to weaken, then he hardens again.*]

CURLEY: Naw, I'm gonna shoot the guts out of that big bastard, I'm gonna get him myself. Come on, you guys.

SLIM [*to* CANDY]: You stay here then, Candy. The rest of us better get goin'. [*They walk out,* SLIM *and* GEORGE *last. Exeunt all but* CANDY. *He squats in the hay, watching the face of* CURLEY'S WIFE.]

CANDY: *Poor bastard.*

CURTAIN

ACT THREE: SCENE II

Evening.

The river bank again.

Light from the setting sun shines on the low brown hills. Among the trees by the river, the shade is deep with evening feeling.

Sounds: distant barking of dogs and the quiet call of quail.

The curtain rises on an empty stage.

There is a sudden whistle of evening wind that stirs the trees and scuds the leaves on the ground.

The stage is still again. LENNIE *enters as silently as a bear. He is bent over and wary. On stage he looks behind him. Then he takes from under his coat the dead pup, lays it on the ground and, going to the river, lies on his stomach and drinks.*

He returns to the dead pup, sits down beside it.

LENNIE: George gonna give me hell . . . I bet. I . . . won't tell him. I'll bury him. [*Begins to scoop a hole in the sand in front of him. Softly.*] But I didn't forget, you bet. I come right here. Hide in the brush an' wait for George. [*Works carefully at his little grave, shaping the hole. At last he picks up the pup and lays it in the hole. Mourning.*] He gonna give me hell. He gonna wish he was alone. [*Adjusts the puppy in the hole, turning it around to make it fit better. Defiantly.*] Well . . . I can go right up in the hills an' find a cave. 'Course I wouldn't never have no ketchup. [*Begins packing sand down carefully about the pup, patting it as he does in beat with his words.*] I'll—go—away—go—away. [*Every word a pat. Fills the grave carefully, smooths the sand over it.*] There now. [*Gathers leaves and scatters them over the place. Gets up on his knees and cocks his head to inspect the job.*] Now. I won't never tell George. [*Sinks back to a sitting position.*] He'll know. He always knows.

Far off sound of voices approaching. They come closer during the scene. Suddenly there is the clicking warning of a cock-quail and then the drum of the flock's wings. GEORGE *enters silently, but hurriedly.*

GEORGE [*in a hoarse whisper*]: Get in the tules—quick.

LENNIE: I ain't done nothing, George. [*The voices are very close.*]

GEORGE [*frantically*]: Get in the tules—damn you. [*Voices are nearly there.* GEORGE *half pushes* LENNIE *down among the tules. The tops rustle showing his crawling progress.*]

WHIT [*offstage*]: There's George. [*Enters.*] Better not get so far ahead. You ain't got a gun. [*Enter* SLIM, CARLSON, BOSS, CURLEY, *and three other ranch hands. They are armed with shotguns and rifles.*]

CARLSON: He musta come this way. Them prints in the sand was aimed this way.

SLIM [*has been regarding* GEORGE]: Now look. We ain't gonna find him stickin' in a bunch this way. We got to spread out.

CURLEY: Brush is pretty thick here. He might be lying in the brush. [*Steps toward the tules.* GEORGE *moves quickly after him.*]

SLIM [*Seeing the move speaks quickly*]: Look—[*pointing*]—

up there's the county road an' open fields an' over there's the highway. Le's spread out an' cover the brush.

BOSS: Slim's right. We got to spread.

SLIM: We better drag up to the roads an' then drag back.

CURLEY: 'Member what I said—shoot for his guts.

SLIM: Okay, move out. Me an' George'll go up to the county road. You guys gets the highway an' drag back.

BOSS: If we get separated, we'll meet here. Remember this place.

CURLEY: All I care is getting the bastard. [*The men move offstage right, talking.* SLIM *and* GEORGE *move slowly upstage listening to the voices that grow fainter and fainter.*]

SLIM [*softly to* GEORGE]: Where is he? [GEORGE *looks at him in the eyes for a long moment. Finally trusts him and points with his thumb toward the tules.*]

SLIM: You want—I should—go away? [GEORGE *nods slowly, looking at the ground.* SLIM *starts away, comes back, tries to say something, instead puts his hand on* GEORGE'S *shoulder for a second, and then hurries off upstage.*]

GEORGE [*moves woodenly toward the bank and the tule clump and sits down*]: Lennie! [*The tules shiver again and* LENNIE *emerges dripping.*]

LENNIE: Where's them guys goin'? [*Long pause.*]

GEORGE: Huntin'.

LENNIE: Whyn't we go with 'em? I like huntin'. [*Waits for an answer.* GEORGE *stares across the river.*] Is it 'cause I done a bad thing?

GEORGE: It don't make no difference.

LENNIE: Is that why we can't go huntin' with them guys?

GEORGE [*woodenly*]: It don't make no difference.... Sit down, Lennie. Right there. [*The light is going now. In the distance there are shouts of men.* GEORGE *turns his head and listens to the shouts.*]

LENNIE: George!

GEORGE: Yeah?

LENNIE: Ain't you gonna give me hell?

GEORGE: Give ya hell?

LENNIE: Sure. . . . Like you always done before. Like—"If I didn' have you I'd take my fifty bucks . . ."

GEORGE [*softly as if in wonder*]: Jesus Christ, Lennie, you can't remember nothing that happens. But you remember every word I say!

LENNIE: Well, ain't you gonna say it?

GEORGE [*reciting*]: "If I was alone I—could live—so easy. [*His voice is monotonous.*] I could get a job and not have no mess. . . ."

LENNIE: Go on, go on! "And when the end of the month come . . ."

GEORGE: "And when the end of the month come, I could take my fifty bucks and go to—a cat-house. . . ."

LENNIE [*eagerly*]: Go on, George, ain't you gonna give me no more hell?

GEORGE: No!

LENNIE: I can go away. I'll go right off in the hills and find a cave if you don't want me.

GEORGE [*speaks as though his lips were stiff*]: No, I want you to stay here with me.

LENNIE [*craftily*]: Then tell me like you done before.

GEORGE: Tell you what?

LENNIE: 'Bout the other guys and about us!

GEORGE [*recites again*]: "Guys like us got no families. They got a little stake and then they blow it in. They ain't got nobody in the world that gives a hoot in hell about 'em!"

LENNIE [*happily*]: "But not *us*." Tell about us now.

GEORGE: "But not us."

LENNIE: "Because . . ."

GEORGE: "Because I got you and . . ."

LENNIE [*triumphantly*]: "And I got you. We got each other," that's what, that gives a hoot in hell about us. [*A breeze blows up the leaves and then they settle back again. There are the shouts of men again. This time closer.*]

GEORGE [*takes off his hat; shakily*]: Take off your hat, Lennie. The air feels fine!

LENNIE [*removes his hat and lays it on the ground in front of him*]: Tell how it's gonna be. [*Again the sound of men.* GEORGE *listens to them.*]

GEORGE: Look acrost the river, Lennie, and I'll tell you like you can almost see it. [LENNIE *turns his head and looks across the river.*] "We gonna get a little place . . . [*Reaches in his side pocket and brings out* CARLSON'S *Luger. Hand and gun lie on the ground behind* LENNIE'S *back. He stares at the back of* LENNIE'S *head at the place where spine and skull are joined. Sounds of men's voices talking offstage.*]

LENNIE: Go on! [GEORGE *raises the gun, but his hand shakes and he drops his hand on to the ground.*] Go on! How's it gonna be? "We gonna get a little place. . . ."

GEORGE [*thickly*]: "We'll have a cow. And we'll have maybe a pig and chickens—and down the flat we'll have a . . . little piece of alfalfa. . . ."

LENNIE [*shouting*]: "For the rabbits!"

GEORGE: "For the rabbits!"

LENNIE: "And I get to tend the rabbits?"

GEORGE: "And you get to tend the rabbits!"

LENNIE [*giggling with happiness*]: "And live on the fat o' the land!"

GEORGE: Yes. [LENNIE *turns his head. Quickly.*] Look over there, Lennie. Like you can really see it.

LENNIE: Where?

GEORGE: Right acrost that river there. Can't you almost see it?

LENNIE [*moving*]: Where, George?

GEORGE: It's over there. You keep lookin', Lennie. Just keep lookin'.

LENNIE: I'm lookin', George. I'm lookin'.

GEORGE: That's right. It's gonna be nice there. Ain't gonna be no trouble, no fights. Nobody ever gonna hurt nobody, or steal from 'em. It's gonna be—nice.

LENNIE: I can see it, George. I can see it! Right over there! I can see it! [GEORGE *fires.* LENNIE *crumples; falls behind the brush. The voices of the men in the distance.*]

CURTAIN

THE MOON IS DOWN

A PLAY IN TWO PARTS

Following is a copy of the original program:

MARTIN BECK THEATRE

BEGINNING TUESDAY, APRIL 7, 1942

OSCAR SERLIN

PRESENTS

JOHN STEINBECK'S

THE MOON IS DOWN

WITH

OTTO KRUGER   RALPH MORGAN

DIRECTED BY CHESTER ERSKIN
PRODUCTION DESIGNED BY HOWARD BAY

CAST

(IN ORDER OF APPEARANCE)

DR. WINTER	Whitford Kane
JOSEPH	Joseph Sweeney
SERGEANT	Edwin Gordon
CAPTAIN BENTICK	John D. Seymour
MAYOR ORDEN	Ralph Morgan
MADAME ORDEN	Leona Powers
CORPORAL	Charles Gordon
COLONEL LANSER	Otto Kruger
GEORGE CORELL	E. J. Ballantine
ANNIE	Jane Seymour
SOLDIER	Kermit Kegley
MAJOR HUNTER	Russell Collins
LIEUTENANT PRACKLE	Carl Gose
CAPTAIN LOFT	Alan Hewitt
LIEUTENANT TONDER	William Eythe
SOLDIER	Victor Thorley
MOLLY MORDEN	Maria Palmer
ALEX MORDEN	Philip Foster
WILL ANDERS	George Keane
TOM ANDERS	LYLE BETTGER

PRODUCTION STAGE MANAGER, B. D. KRANZ

The action of the play occurs in a small mining town.
The time is the present.

PART I

The drawing-room of the Mayor's house.

SCENE I. Morning.

SCENE II. A few days later.

SCENE III. Two days later.

SCENE IV. That evening.

INTERMISSION

PART II

SCENE I. The drawing-room of the Mayor's house. Three months later.

SCENE II. The living-room of Molly Morden's house. The following evening.

SCENE III. The drawing-room. Two weeks later.

SCENE IV. The same. Half an hour later.

PART ONE

PART ONE: SCENE I

SCENE: *The drawing-room of the tiny palace of the* MAYOR *of a small mining town. The room is poor, but has about it a certain official grandeur; tarnished gold chairs with worn tapestry seats and backs, and the slight stuffiness of all official rooms. In the downstage R. wall is a fireplace with coal grate and a mantel of white marble on which there is a large porcelain clock, and behind it a dark frame filled with miniature pictures. Upstage two large windows, and up L., glass-paned doors to vestibule and stairs leading to the upper floor. Down L., a door which it will appear leads to the* MAYOR'S *bedroom. Upstage R., a door which apparently leads to the dining-room, kitchen and stairways in the upper part of the house. The grandeur of the room is carried out with completely useless but very beautiful bric-a-brac on mantel and on tables, and whatever lamps are necessary to light the scene. Altogether it is a warm room which, trying to be stiff and official, has from use become rather comfortable and pleasant. A small coal fire burns in the grate. A brass coal-scuttle stands on the hearth. An upholstered arm-chair stands near the fireplace. A chess game on a small table stands between the arm-chair and a side-chair which faces the arm-chair. In the center of the room is a large sofa with a small table at each end. The* MAYOR'S *desk and chair stand against the L. wall upstage of his bedroom door. On*

this wall hang three gold-framed paintings. R. of the ves-
tibule doors is a large grandfather's clock. In the window
alcove is an elaborate table with a side-chair at its down-
stage side. In this alcove, too, is a gold painted pedestal on
which stands an elaborate silver-leaf vase holder with a glass
vase filled with ferns. Side-chairs are L. of vestibule doors
and down L. facing the sofa. Wall L. of dining-room door
carries a large gold-framed painting. Below it stands a con-
sole table. R. wall below dining-room door carries two small
gold-framed pictures. All the walls except the R. one are
covered with drapes of a dark red and gold figure. A pleas-
ant warm light comes into the room from the outside.

As the curtain rises, DR. WINTER, *bearded, simple and*
benign, is sitting on the sofa. He is the town historian and
physician, and is dressed in a dark suit and very white
linen, but his shoes are heavy and thick-soled. He sits roll-
ing his thumbs over and over in his lap.

JOSEPH, *the serving man of the* MAYOR, *goes about*
straightening furniture, doing little things that by no means
need to be done, and occasionally looking at WINTER.

WINTER [*looking up from his thumbs*]: Eleven o'clock?
JOSEPH [*abstractedly carrying ash-tray from desk to end*
    table L. of sofa]: Yes, sir, the note said eleven.
WINTER [*half-humorously*]: You read the note, Joseph?
JOSEPH [*ignoring the humor, carrying side-chair from L.C.*
    to L. of table U.C.]: No, sir. His Excellency read the note
    to me.
WINTER: He always asks me to come when there's trouble.

JOSEPH *moves about the room, straightening furniture*
he has already straightened. He moves side-chair R.C. to
R. end of table U.C.

JOSEPH: Yes, sir.
WINTER [*amusingly*]: Eleven o'clock. [*He glances at watch*

he has taken from his pocket.] And they'll be here, too. [*Pause.*] A time-minded people, Joseph.

JOSEPH [*not listening*]: Yes, sir.

WINTER: A time-minded people.

JOSEPH: Yes, sir.

WINTER: They hurry to their destiny as though it wouldn't wait.

JOSEPH [*obviously not listening*]: Quite right, sir.

WINTER [*rolling his thumbs rapidly and watching* JOSEPH *discipline the table R. of sofa*]: What's the Mayor doing?

JOSEPH: Dressing to receive the Colonel, sir.

WINTER [*in mock concern*]: And you aren't helping him? He'll be badly dressed by himself.

JOSEPH [*stuffily, crossing to mantel for small ornament which he places on table R. of sofa*]: Madame is helping him. Madame wants him to look his best. She is trimming the hair out of his ears. He won't let me do it. He says it tickles.

WINTER: Of course it tickles.

JOSEPH [*stuffily*]: Madame insists.

WINTER [*rises and crosses to mantel, lighting pipe. As he leaves sofa,* JOSEPH *straightens the pillows on it*]: We're so wonderful. Our country is invaded and Madame is holding the Mayor by the neck and trimming the hair from his ears.

JOSEPH [*sternly, crosses to table U.C., arranging chairs around table R. to L.*]: He was getting shaggy, sir. His eyebrows, too. His Excellency is even more upset about having his eyebrows trimmed than his ears. He says that hurts.

WINTER: It does.

JOSEPH: She wants him to look his best. [JOSEPH *at L. end of table turns sharply to look at* WINTER.]

WINTER [*looking at clock*]: They're early. Let them in, Joseph.

JOSEPH *goes into vestibule. The front door is heard opening. A* SOLDIER *steps in, dressed in a long coat, helmeted and carrying over his arm a submachine gun. He glances quickly about and then steps aside.* CAPTAIN BENTICK *enters and stands in the doorway.*

NOTE *On Uniforms.* Throughout, the uniforms of both soldiers and officers are plain as possible. Rank can be indicated by small colored tabs at the collar, but little else. *Helmets* should be a variation on any obvious shape which will identify these as being soldiers of any known nation.

BENTICK [*looking at* WINTER. BENTICK *is a slightly overdrawn picture of an English gentleman. He has a slouch. His face is red, long nose, but rather pleasant, and he seems as unhappy in his uniform as most British General Officers are.* JOSEPH *follows* BENTICK *in and stands at door*]: Are you Mayor Orden?

WINTER: No. No, I am not.

BENTICK: You are an official?

WINTER [*coming toward him*]: I'm the town doctor. I'm a friend of the Mayor.

BENTICK [*crossing to him*]: Where is Mayor Orden?

JOSEPH *crosses D.L. to watch.*

WINTER: Dressing to receive you, sir. You *are* the Colonel?

BENTICK [*almost embarrassedly*]: I am Captain Bentick. [*He bows and* WINTER *bows slightly back to him.* BENTICK *continues, as though a little embarrassed at what he has to say.*] We search for weapons before the Commanding Officer enters a room. We mean no disrespect, sir. [*Calling to* SERGEANT.] Sergeant . . .

SERGEANT *moves quickly to* JOSEPH *and runs his hands over his pockets.*

SERGEANT: Nothing, sir.

BENTICK [*To* WINTER]: I hope you will pardon us.

SERGEANT *approaches* WINTER, *pats his pockets.*

SERGEANT: Nothing, sir. [*He then crosses to fireplace, examines it, then goes to door R. Looks out.*]

JOSEPH *watches* SERGEANT *and crosses to R. of clock.*

BENTICK [*he takes a card from his pocket, reads it and says*]: I believe there are some firearms here.

WINTER: You are thorough.

SERGEANT *crosses to clock U.L., opens pendulum door and looks inside.*

BENTICK [*crossing to fireplace*]: Yes, we are. We wouldn't have been so successful if we weren't.

WINTER: Do you know where every gun in the town is?

BENTICK: Nearly all, I guess. We had our people working here for quite a long time.

SERGEANT *crosses to* MAYOR'S *desk and looks in drawers.*

WINTER: Working here? Who?

SERGEANT *crosses R. above sofa to door R. and exits.*

BENTICK: Well, the work is done now. It's bound to come out. The man in charge here is named Corell.

JOSEPH *follows* SERGEANT *to door R. Stops to listen for a moment, then exits after* SERGEANT.

WINTER [*unbelieving*]: George Corell?

BENTICK: Yes.

WINTER: I don't believe it. I can't believe it. Why, George had dinner with me on Friday. Why, I've played chess with

George night after night. You must be wrong. Why, he
gave the big shooting match in the hills this morning—
gave the prizes—

BENTICK [*crossing to door R.*]: Yes—that was clever—there
wasn't a soldier in town. [*He exits R.*]

WINTER [*crossing to fireplace*]: George Corell—

The door on the L. opens and MAYOR ORDEN *enters.
He is digging his right ear with his little finger. He is a
fine-looking man of about sixty-five and he seems a little
too common and too simple for the official morning coat
he wears and the gold chain of office around his neck. His
hair has been fiercely brushed, but already a few hairs are
struggling to be free. He has dignity and warmth. Behind
him* MADAME ORDEN *enters. She is small and wrinkled
and fierce, and very proprietary. She considers that she created this man, and ever since he has been trying to get out
of hand. She watches him constantly as the lady shower
of a prize dog watches her entry at a dog show. She comes
up beside the* MAYOR, *takes his hand and pulls his finger
out of his ear and gently puts his hand to his side, the way
she would take a baby's thumb from his mouth.*

MADAME: I don't believe for a moment it hurts that much.
[*She turns to* WINTER.] He won't let me fix his eyebrows.

MAYOR: It hurts.

MADAME: Very well, if you want to look like that. [*She
sees* BENTICK *as he enters R. and crosses C. to sofa. She
crosses to meet him.*] Oh! The Colonel!

SERGEANT *enters after* BENTICK, *crosses U.L.C.* JOSEPH
follows SERGEANT *on. Crosses U.R.*

BENTICK: No, Ma'am . . . I am only preparing for the Colonel. Sergeant! [SERGEANT *comes quickly to* MAYOR *and
runs his hands over his pockets.*] Excuse him, sir . . . it's

the regulations. [SERGEANT *moves toward* MADAME, *but* BENTICK *stops him. She crosses to R. of* BENTICK. *He glances at card in his hand again.*] Your Excellency, I think you have firearms here. Two items, I believe.

MAYOR [*bewildered*]: Firearms! Guns, you mean? Yes, I have a shotgun and a sporting rifle.

BENTICK: Where are these guns, your Excellency?

MAYOR [*rubs his cheek and tries to think*]: Why, I think— [*He turns to* MADAME.]—Aren't they in the back of that cabinet in the bedroom, with the walking sticks?

MADAME: I don't know why you insist on keeping them in the bedroom. You never use them.

BENTICK: Sergeant. [SERGEANT *quickly goes offstage to bedroom.* MADAME *follows him off.*] It's an unpleasant duty. I'm sorry.

MAYOR [*deprecatingly*]: You know I don't hunt very much any more. I always think I'm going to, and then the season opens and I don't get out. I guess I don't take the pleasure in it I used to.

SERGEANT *re-enters, carrying a double-barrelled shotgun and a rather nice sporting rifle with a shoulder strap. He exits into vestibule.* MADAME *enters from bedroom after* SERGEANT.

BENTICK: Thank you, your Excellency. [*Crossing to her.*] Thank you, Madame. [*He turns and bows slightly to* WINTER.] Thank you, Doctor. Colonel Lanser will be here directly. Good morning!

MAYOR: Good morning.

BENTICK *exits by front door. Front door closes.*

MADAME [*crossing U.C.*]: For a moment I thought he was the Colonel.

MAYOR *crosses L. to desk.*

WINTER [*sardonically, crossing to sofa, sits*]: No, he is just protecting the Colonel.

MADAME [*thinking*]: I wonder how many officers will come? [*She looks over at* JOSEPH *and sees that he is shamelessly eavesdropping. She shakes her head at him and frowns and he exits R. She moves chess-table to L. of arm-chair.*] I don't know whether it would be correct to offer them tea or a glass of wine. It is so difficult to plan, when you don't know.

WINTER [*shakes his head and smiles and says in mock seriousness*]: It's been so long since we've been invaded, or invaded anyone else. I just don't know what's correct.

MAYOR: We won't offer them anything. I don't think the people would like it. *I* don't want to drink wine with them. [*Sits desk chair.*]

MADAME [*appealing to* WINTER]: Didn't people in the old days . . . leaders, that is . . . compliment each other . . . take a glass of wine—?

WINTER [*nodding*]: Yes, they did. Rulers used to play at war the way Englishmen play at hunting. When the fox was dead, they got together at a hunt breakfast. The Mayor is right, Madame. The town wouldn't want him to drink wine with the invader.

MADAME [*acidly, as she takes ornament* JOSEPH *set on table R. of sofa, back to mantel*]: They are all down listening to the music. Annie told me they were. Why shouldn't we keep proper decencies alive?

During her speech the MAYOR *has appeared to be coming out of a dream. He looks steadily at* MADAME *and then says sharply.*

MAYOR [*rises, crosses L.C.*]: Madame, I think with your permission we will not have wine! [*She crosses to R. of sofa.*] The people are confused. We have lived at peace so long they don't quite believe in war. Six town boys were

murdered this morning. We will have no hunt breakfast.
The people do not fight wars for sport.

MADAME [*in disbelief, crossing in above sofa*]: Murdered?

MAYOR [*bitterly*]: Our twelve soldiers were at the shooting
match in the hills. They saw the parachutes and they came
back. At the bend in the road by Toller's farm the machine
guns opened on them and six were killed.

MADAME [*excitedly, crossing to him*]: Which ones were
killed? Annie's sister's boy was there.

MAYOR: I don't know which ones were killed. [*He looks at*
WINTER.] I don't even know how many soldiers are here.
[*Crossing to sofa, sits L. of* WINTER.] . . . Do you know
how many men the invader has?

WINTER [*shrugging*]: Not many, I think. Not over two hundred and fifty. But all with those little machine guns.

MAYOR: Have you heard anything about the rest of the
country? Here there were parachutes, a little transport. It
happened so quickly. [WINTER *raises his shoulders and
drops them. The* MAYOR *says, rather hopelessly.*] Was
there no resistance anywhere?

WINTER *again shrugs his shoulders.*

WINTER: I don't know. The wires are cut. There is no
news.

MAYOR: And our soldiers . . . ?

WINTER: I don't know.

JOSEPH [*enters from R., crosses D. to sofa*]: I heard . . .
that is, Annie heard . . . six of our men were killed by
the machine guns. Annie heard three were wounded and
captured.

MAYOR: But there were twelve.

JOSEPH: Annie heard three escaped.

MAYOR [*sharply*]: Which ones escaped?

JOSEPH: I don't know, sir. Annie didn't hear.

MADAME [*crossing R. to arm-chair*]: Joseph, when they

come, don't stay in the room all the time. Stay close to your bell. We might want something. [*He starts for door.* MAYOR *rises, crosses to desk.* MADAME *looks at* JOSEPH *critically.*] And put on your other coat, Joseph . . . [*He stops.*] . . . the one with the buttons. [*She sits arm-chair.* JOSEPH *starts again. Again she inspects* JOSEPH.] Joseph, when you finish what you are told to do, go out of the room. It makes a bad impression when you just stand around listening. It's provincial.

JOSEPH: Yes, Madame. [*He starts again for door.*]

MADAME: We won't serve wine, Joseph. [*He stops.*] But you might have some cigarettes handy . . . in that little silver conserve box. [*He starts.*] When you light the Colonel's cigarette, don't strike the match on your shoe. Strike it on the match-box.

JOSEPH [*coming to her L.*]: Yes, Madame. They won't strike on the shoe, Madame. They are safety matches.

MADAME: Well, strike them on the box, then.

WINTER *takes out his watch.*

JOSEPH: Yes, Madame. [*He exits R.*]

MADAME: And don't forget His Excellency's coffee. [*She rises and exits R.*]

MAYOR, *unbuttoning his coat, takes out his big gold watch, crosses to sofa.*

WINTER: What time have you now?

MAYOR: Five of eleven.

They place their watches back in pockets.

WINTER: Do you want me to go?

MAYOR [*a little startled*]: Oh, no, please stay. I'm nervous. I need you to stay.

WINTER [*rises, crosses to fireplace*]: You always send for me when there's trouble.

Marching feet can be heard approaching the house.

MAYOR [*chuckling*]: Yes, I do, don't I?

MADAME [*enters from R., excitedly, crosses to windows.* MAYOR *rises, crosses to desk*]: Here they come. I hope not too many try to crowd in here at once. It isn't a very big room. [MADAME *crosses L. to* MAYOR.]

JOSEPH *enters from R. buttoning his coat, hurrying to the vestibule, exits U.L.*

WINTER [*sardonically*]: Madame would prefer the hall of mirrors at Versailles?

MADAME [*pinching her lips, looking about*]: It's a very small room.

Outside is heard the command "Company halt!" The marching stops. A knock on the outside door is heard.

CORPORAL [*offstage*]: Colonel Lanser's compliments . . . Colonel Lanser requests an audience with His Excellency. [*The helmeted* CORPORAL *steps inside, looks quickly about and then stands aside, front of clock U.L.C.*]

A second helmeted FIGURE *steps into the room, his rank showing only on his shoulder. He, too, looks quickly about. The* COLONEL *is a middle-aged man, gray and hard and tired-looking. He has the square shoulders of a soldier, but his eyes lack the blank wall of a soldier's man.*

COLONEL LANSER [*after taking off his helmet, with a quick bow*]: Your Excellency. [*Bows to* MADAME.] Madame . . . [LANSER *looks questioningly at* WINTER.]

MAYOR [*fingering his chain of office*]: This is Dr. Winter.

LANSER [*courteously*]: An official?

MAYOR: A doctor, sir, and the local historian.

LANSER [*bows slightly, crossing to C.*]: Dr. Winter. I do not mean to be impertinent, this will be a page in your history, perhaps.

WINTER [*smiling*]: Many pages, perhaps.

GEORGE CORELL *enters quickly, places his coat and hat on chair U.L. corner, steps down to R. of* MAYOR. JOSEPH *follows* CORELL *on, closes doors and exits R.*

LANSER [*turning slightly toward his companion*]: I think you know Mr. Corell! [*Crosses U.R. above sofa.*]

MAYOR: George Corell? Of course we know him. How are you, George?

CORELL: Good morning, sir. There are changes this morning.

WINTER [*cutting in*]: Your Excellency—I think you should know this. Our friend, George Corell, is a traitor.

MAYOR: What do you mean, a traitor?

LANSER *crosses to table U.C., places helmet on table.*

WINTER [*crossing to arm-chair R.—sits*]: He prepared for this invasion. He sent our troops into the hills so they would be out of the way. He listed every firearm in the town. God knows what else he has done. . . .

CORELL [*crossing to* WINTER]: Doctor, you don't understand. This thing was bound to come. It's a good thing. You don't understand it yet, but when you do, you will thank me. The democracy was rotten and inefficient. Things will be better now. Believe me. [*Almost fanatic in his belief.*] When you understand the new order you will know I am right.

MAYOR [*as though he had not heard the argument, turns to* MADAME]: George Corell—a traitor—?

CORELL [*impatiently, crossing to front of sofa*]: I work for what I believe in. That's an honorable thing.

MAYOR [*crossing to* CORELL]: This isn't true—George— [*Almost pleading.*] George—you've sat at my table—on Madame's right—we've played chess together. This isn't true, George—?

CORELL [*sits sofa*]: I work for what I believe in. You will agree with me when you understand.

There is a long silence during which MAYOR'S *face grows tight and formal and his whole body becomes rigid.*

MAYOR [*crossing to desk*]: I don't wish to speak in this gentleman's presence. [*Sits desk chair.*]

CORELL [*rises*]: You have no right to say this. [*Crosses L. to* MAYOR.] I am a soldier like the rest. I just don't wear a uniform.

MAYOR: I don't wish to speak in this gentleman's presence.

LANSER: Will you leave us now, Mr. Corell?

CORELL: I have a right to be here.

LANSER [*sharply*]: Do you out-rank me?

CORELL: Oh! No, sir.

LANSER: Please go, Mr. Corell.

For a moment CORELL *looks at the* MAYOR *and his face is angry, then he turns and goes out the door.*

WINTER [*smiles and chuckles*]: That's worth a paragraph for my history!

LANSER: There are some things we must discuss—first—

MAYOR *rises. Door to R. opens and straw-haired, red-eyed* ANNIE *enters, crossing R.C.*

ANNIE: There's soldiers on the back porch, Madame. Just standing there.

LANSER: It's just military procedure. They won't come in.

MADAME [*coldly*]: Annie, in the future if you have anything to say, let Joseph bring the message.

ANNIE [*defiantly*]: I didn't know but they'd try to get in. They smelled the coffee.

MADAME [*coldly*]: Annie!   ·

ANNIE [*still belligerently*]: Yes, Madame—[*She looks at* LANSER.]—they smelled the coffee. [*She exits R. and closes door.*]

MADAME *sits desk chair.*

LANSER [*crossing around R. of sofa*]: May I sit down, Your Excellency? We've been a long time without sleep.

MAYOR: Yes. . . . Yes, of course, sit down.

He sits L. end sofa, LANSER *R. end sofa.*

LANSER: We want to get along as well as we can. You see, sir, this is more a business venture than anything else. We need your coal mine here, and the fishing. We want to get along with just as little friction as possible.

MAYOR: We've had no news. Can you tell me—what about the rest of the country? What has happened?

LANSER: All taken. It was well planned.

MAYOR [*insistently*]: Was there no resistance . . . anywhere?

LANSER [*looking at him almost compassionately*]: Yes, there was some resistance. I wish there hadn't been. It only caused bloodshed. We'd planned very carefully.

MAYOR [*sticking to his point*]: But there *was* resistance?

LANSER: Yes. . . . And it was foolish to resist. Just as here, it was destroyed instantly. It was sad and foolish to resist.

WINTER [*who has caught some of the* MAYOR'S *anxious-ness about the point*]: Yes . . . foolish, but they resisted.

LANSER: Only a few, and they are gone. The people as a whole are quiet.

WINTER: But the people don't know yet what has happened.

LANSER [*a little sternly*]: They are discovering now. They won't be foolish again. [*His voice changes, takes on a business-like tone.*] I must get to business. I am very tired. Before I can sleep, I must make my arrangements. [*He sits forward.*] The coal from this mine must come out of the ground and be shipped. We have the technicians with us. The local people will continue to work the mine. Is that clear? We do not wish to be harsh.

MAYOR: Yes, that's clear enough. But suppose we don't want to work the mine?

LANSER [*tightly*]: I hope you will want to, because you *must*.

MAYOR: And if we won't?

LANSER [*rising*]: You *must*! [*Crossing to R. end sofa.*] This is an orderly people. They don't want trouble. [*He waits for the* MAYOR'S *reply, and none comes.*] Isn't that so, sir?

MAYOR: I don't know. They're orderly under our government. I don't know what they'll be under yours. We've built our government over a long time.

LANSER [*quickly*]: We know that. We're going to keep your government. You will still be the Mayor. You will give the orders, you will penalize and reward. Then we won't have trouble.

MAYOR [*looking helplessly at* WINTER]: What do you think?

WINTER: I don't know. I'd expect trouble. This might be a bitter people.

MAYOR: I don't know, either. [*He turns to* LANSER.] Perhaps you know, sir. Or maybe it might be different from anything you know. Some accept leaders and obey them. But my people elected me. They made me and they can

unmake me! Perhaps they will do that, when they think
I've gone over to you.

LANSER [*ominously*]: You will be doing them a service if
you keep them in order.

MAYOR: A service?

LANSER [*crossing to front of sofa—sits*]: It's your duty to
protect them. They'll be in danger if they are rebellious. If
they work they will be safe.

MAYOR: But suppose they don't want to be safe?

LANSER: Then you must think for them.

MAYOR [*a little proudly*]: They don't like to have others
think for them. Maybe they are different from your
people?

JOSEPH *enters quickly, crosses D.R., leans forward burst-
ing to speak.*

MADAME [*rises, steps in*]: What is it, Joseph? Get the silver
box of cigarettes.

JOSEPH: Pardon, Your Excellency.

MAYOR: What do you want, Joseph?

JOSEPH [*excitedly*]: It's Annie, sir.

MADAME: What's the matter with her?

JOSEPH: Annie doesn't like soldiers on the back porch.

LANSER: Are they making trouble?

JOSEPH: They're looking through the door at Annie, sir.
She hates that.

LANSER [*sighing*]: They are carrying out orders. They're
doing no harm.

MAYOR *looks at* MADAME *helplessly.*

JOSEPH: Well, Annie hates to be stared at, sir. She's getting
angry.

MADAME: Joseph, you tell Annie to mind her temper.

JOSEPH [*with a gesture of resignation*]: Yes, Madame. [*He turns, shrugs at* WINTER, *then exits R.*]

MADAME *crosses to desk chair, sits.*

LANSER [*his eyes dropping with weariness*]: There is one other thing, Your Excellency. Will it be possible for my staff and me to stay here?

MAYOR [*uneasily, a look at* MADAME]: It's a small place. There are larger and more comfortable houses.

LANSER: It isn't that, sir. We have found that when a staff lives under the roof of the local authority, there is more . . . tranquility.

MAYOR [*a little angrily*]: You mean . . . the people sense there is collaboration.

LANSER: Yes, I suppose that's it. [JOSEPH *comes in with silver box of cigarettes, opens it ostentatiously in front of* LANSER. MADAME *rises to watch. He takes one and* JOSEPH *just as ostentatiously lights it, showing* MADAME *the match he struck on box before lighting cigarette.* LANSER *inhales deeply.* JOSEPH *leaves box on table R. of sofa, exits R.*]

MAYOR [*looks hopelessly at* WINTER *and* WINTER *can offer him nothing but a wry smile.* MAYOR *speaks softly*]: Am I permitted . . . to refuse?

LANSER [*taking a deep puff on cigarette*]: I'm sorry. No.

MAYOR: The people will not like it.

LANSER [*as though he speaks to a recalcitrant child*]: Always the people. The people are disarmed. They have no say in this.

MAYOR [*shaking his head*]: You do not know, sir!

From door R. come the following sounds:

FIRST SOLDIER: Look out!

SECOND SOLDIER: It's boiling!

JOSEPH *enters running.*

THIRD SOLDIER: Jump!

*The splash of water, the clang of a pan, and a sharp cry
from a soldier.*

JOSEPH [*excitedly*]: Madame! Annie!

MADAME [*rises, crosses above sofa, running*]: Annie! [*Exits
R.*]

MAYOR [*crossing above sofa, to* JOSEPH]: Was anyone
hurt?

JOSEPH: The water was boiling! [*Exits R.*]

From door R. comes the following:

ANNIE: You get out of here! Out of my kitchen! I'll show
you!

MADAME: Annie, you behave yourself!

FIRST SOLDIER: Grab her! Get hold of her!

MADAME: Annie!

ANNIE: Let go of me!

MADAME: Annie, you stop that!

*A sharp thud of someone being thrown to the floor, and a
cry from a soldier as though he had been bitten.*

LANSER [*getting up heavily, crosses to desk, speaks angrily*]:
Have you no control over your servants, sir?

MAYOR [*smiling*]: Very little. Annie is a good cook when
she's happy.

LANSER [*wearily*]: We just want to do our job. You must
discipline your cook.

MAYOR: I can't. She'll quit.

LANSER: This is an emergency. She can't quit.

WINTER [*very much amused*]: Then she'll throw water.

The door, R., opens and a SOLDIER *enters, crosses D.R.*

SOLDIER: Shall I arrest this woman, sir?

LANSER: Was anyone hurt?

SOLDIER: Yes, sir, scalded, and one man bitten. We are holding her down, sir.

LANSER [*helplessly, leans against desk*]: Oh! Release her and go outside.

SOLDIER: Very good, sir. [*crosses R. to door.*]

LANSER: Off the porch.

SOLDIER *exits and closes door behind him.*

LANSER: I could lock her up. I could have her shot.

MAYOR: Then we'd have no cook.

LANSER [*putting out cigarette in desk ash-tray*]: Our instructions are to get along with your people. I'm very tired, sir. I must have some sleep. Please cooperate with us for the good of all.

MAYOR [*thoughtfully*]: I don't know. The people are confused and so am I!

LANSER: But will you try to cooperate?

MAYOR [*slowly, crossing to front sofa*]: I don't know. When the town makes up its mind what it wants to do I will probably do that. [*Sits sofa.*]

LANSER: You're the authority.

MAYOR: Authority is in the town. That means we cannot act as quickly as you can . . . but when the direction is set . . . we act all together. I don't know . . . yet!

LANSER: I hope we can get along together. I hope we can depend on you to help. Look at it realistically. There's nothing you can do to stop us. And I don't like to think of the means the military must take to keep order. [*Crosses U.C. to table for helmet.*]

MAYOR *is silent, looking at floor.*

MADAME [*enter from R. with cup of coffee, crosses to R. of* MAYOR]: She's all right. [*Hands him cup.*]

LANSER *crosses D.L., puts on helmet.*

MAYOR [*taking cup*]: Thank you, my dear.
LANSER: I hope we can depend on you.
MAYOR: I don't know—yet.

LANSER *bows, turns sharply, exits U.L., followed by* CORPORAL. MADAME *sits R. of* MAYOR *on sofa, straightens his hair.*

CURTAIN

PART ONE: SCENE II

SCENE: *The same room a few days later. Piled military equipment and canvas-wrapped bundles are lying around. The sofa and end-tables as well as the chess-table, pedestal and vase of ferns have been removed. The 3 gold-framed pictures that hung above the* MAYOR'S *desk have been taken down. The drapes and curtains which hung at the windows have been removed. On the mantel stands only a clock and an ash-tray. The* MAYOR'S *desk has maps, a microscope, several specimens of rock and ore. At the windows are three odd chairs. Three more chairs are placed at the table in C. of room. This is the same table that was at the windows in the preceding scene.*

Since most of the staff enter this scene, they might be described thus:

MAJOR HUNTER, *the second in command, is a short wide-shouldered mining engineer . . . a man of figures and a formula. If there had been no war, no one would have thought of making a soldier of him. None of the humor, or the music, or the mysticism of higher mathematics ever entered his head. His drawing-board and his geologic hammer were his most important possessions. He had been married twice, and he did not know why each of his wives became very nervous before she left him.* HUNTER'S *brows are heavy and his eyes small and bright and wide-set.*

CAPTAIN BENTICK, *who comes into the scene only as a corpse, was a family man. A lover of dogs and pink children and Christmas. He was too old to be a Captain, but a curious lack of ambition has kept him in that rank. When there is no war, he admires British country gentlemen very much, wears English clothes, keeps English dogs, smokes a special pipe mixture sent him from London, in an English pipe. He subscribes to those country magazines which extol flower gardening, and continually argues about the merit of English and Gordon Setters. Once he wrote a letter to the* Times *concerning grass drying in the Midlands. He signed it, "Edmund Twitchel, Esquire" and the* Times *had printed it.*

CAPTAIN LOFT *is truly a military man. As much a Captain as one can imagine. He lives and breathes his Captaincy. He has no unmilitary moments. He can click his heels as perfectly as a dancer does. He knows every kind of military courtesy, and insists on using it all. Generals are afraid of him because he knows more about the deportment of soldiers than they do. He believes that a soldier is the highest development of animal life, and if he considers God at all, he thinks of him as an old and honored General, retired and gray, living among remembered battles.*

LIEUTENANT PRACKLE *is an undergraduate . . . a snot-nose; a lieutenant trained in the politics of the day, he believes the great new system invented by a genius so great that he has never bothered to verify its results.* LIEUTENANT PRACKLE *is a devil with women. If he lived in America he might well be giving his all every Saturday to his Alma Mater, for war to him is rather like a football game, and so far he has enjoyed it immensely. He is a sentimental young man, and he considers himself a cynical one. He carries a lock of hair in his watch, which is constantly getting loose and clogging the balance wheel.* PRACKLE *is a pleasant dancing partner, but nevertheless he can scold like the*

*leader, can brood like the leader; he hates degenerate art,
and has destroyed several canvasses with his own hands.*
PRACKLE *has several blonde sisters, of whom he is proud
and about whom he is sensitive. He has caused a commo-
tion on occasion when he thought they were insulted. His
sisters are a little upset about it, because they are afraid
someone might set out to prove the insults, which would
not be hard to do.* LIEUTENANT PRACKLE *once spent
two weeks' furlough attempting to seduce* LIEUTENANT
TONDER'S *blonde sister, a buxom girl who loved to be
seduced by older men who did not muss her hair as*
LIEUTENANT PRACKLE *did.*

LIEUTENANT TONDER *is a different kind of sopho-
more. A dark and bitter and cynical poet, who dreams of
the perfect ideal love of elevated young men for poor girls.
Once he wooed and won a beautiful and smelly waif, and
that was before the application of Sulphanilamide. He
broods often on death, his own particularly, lighted by a
fair setting sun which glints on broken military equipment,
his men standing silently around him, with low-sunk heads,
while over a fat cloud gallop the Valkyrie to the thunderous
strains of Wagnerian music. And he has his dying words
ready to speak.*

*There are the men of the staff, each one playing war as
children play run-sheep-run, and their wars so far have
been play . . . fine weapons and fine planning against
unarmed, planless and surprised enemies. Under pressure
they were capable of courage or cowardice, as anyone is.*

COLONEL LANSER, *among them all, knows what war
really is. He had been in Belgium and France twenty years
before, and he tries not to think what he knows; that war is
hatred and treachery, the muddling of incompetent generals, torture and killing and sick tiredness, until at last it is
over and nothing has changed except for new weariness
and new hatreds.* LANSER *is a soldier; given orders to*

carry out, he will carry them out. And he will try to put aside his own sick memories of war.

As the curtain rises it is morning. R. of the large center table MAJOR HUNTER *sits. He is balancing his drawing board against the edge of the table and against his lap. He works with a T-Square triangle and drawing pencil. The drawing-board is unsteady and unsatisfactory to work on. Attempting to draw a line, his pencil slips.*

HUNTER [*calling sharply*]: Prackle, Lieutenant Prackle!

The bedroom door opens, PRACKLE *comes out. His tunic is off, and half his face is covered with shaving cream. He holds the shaving brush in his hand.*

PRACKLE: Yes, Major.

HUNTER [*jiggling his drawing-board*]: Hasn't the tripod for my board turned up in the baggage yet?

PRACKLE [*crossing in*]: I don't know. I didn't look.

HUNTER: Well, look now, will you? It's bad enough to have to work in this light. I'll have to draw this again before I ink it.

PRACKLE [*crossing to door L.*]: I'll find it as soon as I finish shaving.

HUNTER [*irritably*]: It seems to me this railroad siding is more important than your looks. See if there is a tripod case in there.

PRACKLE *exits L. The door to stairway opens and* CAPTAIN LOFT *enters.*

LOFT [*wears helmet, a pair of field-glasses, side-arm, and various little leather cases strung all over him. He begins to remove his equipment as soon as he enters*]: You know Bentick is crazy. He was going on duty in a fatigue cap, right down the street. [*He puts his glasses on table, takes off his helmet and gas-mask bag. A little pile of equipment begins to heap up on the table.*]

HUNTER: Don't leave that stuff there. I have to work here. [LOFT *places his things on chair above table.*] Why shouldn't he wear a fatigue cap? There hasn't been any trouble. I get sick of these damn tin hats. You can't see out from under them.

LOFT [*grimly. Draws himself up when he speaks, as though he were making a report*]: It's bad business to leave the helmet off. Bad for the people here. We must maintain a military standard of alertness, and never vary it.

HUNTER: What makes you think so?

LOFT [*draws himself a little higher, thins his mouth with certainty. Sooner or later everyone wants to punch* LOFT *in the nose for his sureness about things*]: I don't think it. I was paraphrasing Manual X12 on Deportment in Occupied Countries. It is very carefully worked out. The leaders have considered everything. [*He starts to say "you," and then changes it to*—] Every soldier should read X12 very carefully. [*Sits chair L. of table.*]

HUNTER: I wonder whether the man who wrote it was ever in an occupied country. These people seem harmless enough.

PRACKLE *comes through door and crosses to R. window, his face still half-covered with dry shaving soap. He carries a brown canvas tube and an iron tripod base.*

PRACKLE: Here it is, Major.

HUNTER: Unpack it, will you, and set it up.

PRACKLE *opens bag, takes out a metal rod and puts it in the base.* HUNTER *takes his drawing equipment to chair at window.* LIEUTENANT TONDER *enters from R. with cup of coffee, crosses to chair vacated by* HUNTER, *sits and looks at the plan on board.*

LOFT: You have soap on your face, Lieutenant.

PRACKLE: Yes, sir. I was shaving when the Major asked me to get the tripod.

LOFT: Better get it off; the Colonel might see you.

PRACKLE: Oh, he wouldn't mind; he doesn't care about that.

LOFT: Better wipe it off.

PRACKLE *exits* L. TONDER *is looking at* HUNTER'S *board and points to a drawing in the corner of the board.* HUNTER *sets a chair at tripod.*

TONDER: That's a nice-looking bridge, Major, but where are we going to build a bridge?

HUNTER [*crosses to table for board, looks down at drawing and then at* TONDER]: Huh? Oh, that isn't any bridge we're going to build. Up here is the work drawing. [*Takes board to tripod.*]

TONDER [*rises, crosses U. to window*]: Well, what are you doing with the bridge, then?

HUNTER [*a little embarrassedly, as he readies his board for work, sitting behind it*]: I was just playing with that. You know in my backyard at home I've got a model railroad line. I was going to bridge a little creek for it. Brought the line right down to the creek, but I never did get the bridge built. I thought I would kind of work it out while I was away.

PRACKLE *enters buttoning his tunic. He has a folded rotogravure page from his pocket. It is a picture of an actress, or any one of a number of girls who are all legs, and dress and eyelashes. A well-developed blonde in black open-work stockings, and a low bodice. She peeps over a black lace fan.* TONDER *crosses L.C.*

PRACKLE [*holding her up*]: Isn't she something?

LOFT *glances at picture then turns back to his work at table.* HUNTER *goes on drawing.*

TONDER [*looks critically at picture*]: I don't like her.

PRACKLE: What don't you like about her?

TONDER: I just don't like her. [*Crossing R. below table to arm-chair at fireplace.*] What do you want her picture for?

PRACKLE: Because I do like her. I bet you do, too.

TONDER: No, I don't.

PRACKLE: You mean to say you wouldn't go out with her if you could?

TONDER: No. [*Sits arm-chair.*]

PRACKLE: You're just crazy. [*Goes to wall above desk L.*] I'm just going to stick her up here and let you brood about her for a while. [*He nails picture on wall with a rock from desk.*]

LOFT [*busy with his work*]: I don't think that looks very well out here, Lieutenant. It would make a bad impression on the local people. Better take it down.

HUNTER [*looks up from his board for the first time*]: Take what down? [*He follows their eyes to picture.*] Who's that?

PRACKLE: She's an actress. [*Sits desk chair admiring picture.*]

HUNTER: Oh, you know her?

TONDER: She's a tramp.

HUNTER: Oh, then you know her?

PRACKLE [*he seems only now to have understood* TONDER. *Rises, steps in*]: Say, how do you know she's a tramp?

TONDER: She looks like a tramp. [*Rises, places cup on mantel.*]

PRACKLE: Do you know her?

TONDER: No, and I don't want to. [*Crosses to R. of* HUNTER, *watching him work.*]

PRACKLE [*begins to say*]: Then, how do you know . . .?

LOFT [*breaking in, looking at him*]: Take the picture down. Put it up over your bed if you want to. This is official here. [PRACKLE *looks at him mutinously.*] That's an order.

PRACKLE *takes down picture, sits desk chair, looking at it.*

TONDER [*looking over* HUNTER'S *shoulder again*]: What's that?

HUNTER [*coming slowly out of his work*]: That's a new line I'm building from the mine to the ships. Got to get the coal moving. It's a big job. I'm glad the people here are calm and sensible.

LOFT: They are calm and sensible because *we* are calm and sensible. I think we can take credit for that. That is why I keep harping on procedure. It is very carefully worked out.

PRACKLE [*tries cheerily to change the subject to save his face*]: There are some pretty girls in this town, too. As soon as we get settled down, I'm going to get acquainted with a few.

LOFT: You'd better read X12. There is a chapter dealing with sexual matters.

PRACKLE *folds picture and puts it in his pocket. Door U.L. opens and* LANSER *enters, removing his coat as he comes in. His staff gives him military courtesy, but it is not rigid.*

LANSER: Captain Loft, will you go down and relieve Bentick at the mine. He isn't feeling well. Says he is dizzy.

PRACKLE *takes his coat and helmet into bedroom L.* TONDER *crosses to chair at window, sits looking out.*

LOFT [*getting into his coat and equipment*]: Yes, sir. May I suggest, sir, that I only recently came off duty?

LANSER [*inspecting him closely*]: I hope you don't mind going?

LOFT: Not at all, sir. I just mentioned it for the record.

LANSER [*relaxing and chuckling. Sits against desk*]: You like to be mentioned in the record.

LOFT: It does no harm, sir.

LANSER [*lighting cigarette*]: And when you have enough mentions there will be a little dangler on your chest.

LOFT: They are the milestones in a military career, sir.

LANSER: Yes, I guess they are. But . . . they won't be the ones you'll remember.

LOFT: Sir?

LANSER: You'll know what I mean later . . . perhaps.

LOFT [*putting on his equipment rapidly*]: Yes sir. [*He goes out doors U.L.*]

LANSER [*watches him go with a little amusement. Quietly*]: There is a born soldier.

HUNTER [*poises his pencil and looks up from board*]: A born ass.

LANSER [*crossing to table—looks at reports*]: No. He is being a soldier the way another man would be a politician. [PRACKLE *enters from L.*] He'll be on the General Staff before long. He'll look down on the war from above and so he'll always love it.

PRACKLE: When do you think the war will be over, sir?

LANSER: Over?

TONDER *turns to them.*

PRACKLE [*stepping in*]: How soon will we win?

LANSER [*shaking his head*]: Oh, I don't know. The enemy is still in the world.

PRACKLE: But we'll lick them.

LANSER [*crossing to fireplace*]: Yes?

PRACKLE: Won't we?

LANSER [*smiling a little sadly*]: Yes ... Yes ... [*Turns to him.*] We always do.

PRACKLE [*excitedly. Crosses to table, sits chair L. of table*]: Well, if it is quiet around Christmas, do you think there might be some furloughs?

TONDER *rises, crosses D. to table.*

LANSER: I don't know. The orders will have to come from home. Do you want to get home for Christmas?

PRACKLE: Well, I'd like to.

LANSER: Maybe you will. ... Maybe you will.

TONDER: We won't drop out of this occupation, will we, sir ... after the war is over?

LANSER: I don't know. Why?

TONDER [*sits chair above table*]: Well, it's a nice country. Nice people. Our men, some of them, might even settle here.

LANSER [*jokingly*]: You've seen a place you like?

TONDER [*a little embarrassed*]: Well, there are some beautiful little farms here. If four or five of them were thrown together, it would make a nice place to settle.

LANSER: You have no family land at home, then?

TONDER: Not any more, sir. The inflation took it away.

LANSER [*tiring now of talking to children*]: Ah, well. We still have a war to fight. We still have coal to ship. [*Crossing to HUNTER.*] Suppose we wait until it is over, before we build up estates. Hunter, your steel will be in tomorrow. You can get your tracks started this week.

A knock at door U.L. CORPORAL enters.

CORPORAL: Mr. Corell wishes to see you, sir.

LANSER: Send him in. [CORPORAL *exits.* LANSER,

speaking to the others, crossing to R. end of table.] He worked hard here for us. We might have some trouble with him.

TONDER: Didn't he do a good job?

LANSER: Yes, he did. But he won't be popular with the people here. [*Sits chair R. of table.*] I wonder if he will be popular with us.

TONDER: He deserves credit.

LANSER: Yes, I suppose he does. But that won't make him popular.

CORELL [*comes in rubbing his hands. He radiates good will and good fellowship. He is dressed in a black business suit. On his head there is a patch of white bandage, stuck into his hair with a cross of adhesive tape. He crosses D. to L. of* PRACKLE]: Good morning, Colonel. I should have called yesterday, after the little misunderstanding. But I know how busy you are.

LANSER: Good morning. [*With a circular gesture of his hand.*] This is my staff, Mr. Corell.

CORELL: Fine boys. [*Slaps* PRACKLE *on the back, who rises and exits L.* CORELL *crosses D.L.*] They did a good job. I did my best to prepare for them.

HUNTER *takes out an inking pen, dips it, and begins to ink in his drawing.*

LANSER [*rises, crosses R. to fireplace.* CORELL *crosses to chair L. of table*]: You did very well. I wish we hadn't killed those six men, though.

CORELL: Well, six men isn't much for a town like this, with a coal mine, too.

LANSER [*sternly*]: I don't mind killing people if that finishes it. [*Turns to him.*] But sometimes it doesn't finish it.

CORELL [*looking sideways at* TONDER *and* HUNTER]: Perhaps if we could talk alone, Colonel—?

LANSER: Yes, if you wish. Lieutenant Tonder, will you go to your room, please. [TONDER *rises, bows, exits L.* CORELL *then gestures toward* HUNTER.] Major Hunter is working. He doesn't hear anything when he's working. [HUNTER *looks up from his board, smiles quietly and looks down again.* LANSER, *not quite at his ease, crossing in to R.C.*] Well, here we are. Won't you sit down?

CORELL: Thank you, Sir. [CORELL *takes off coat and hat, places them on chair above table, sits down chair L. of table.*]

LANSER [*studies bandage on* CORELL'S *head. Speaks bluntly*]: Have they tried to kill you already?

CORELL [*fingers the bandage*]: This? Oh, no. This was a stone that fell from the cliff in the hills this morning.

LANSER: You are sure it wasn't thrown?

CORELL: What do you mean? These aren't fierce people. They haven't had a war for a hundred years. They've forgotten about fighting.

LANSER [*crossing L. to desk*]: Well, you've lived among them, you ought to know. But if you are safe, these people are different from any in the world. I've helped to occupy countries before. I was in Belgium twenty years ago, and in France. [*Sits against desk, shakes head a little as though to clear it. To* CORELL, *gruffly.*] You did a good job. I have mentioned your work in my report.

CORELL [*turns to him*]: Thank you, sir. I did my best.

LANSER [*a little wearily, places foot on desk chair*]: Well, now what shall we do with you? Would you like to go back to the Capitol? You can go in a coal barge if you are in a hurry, or in a destroyer if you want to wait.

CORELL: I don't want to go back. My place is here.

LANSER: I haven't very many men. I can't give you a bodyguard.

CORELL: But I don't need a bodyguard. I tell you these are not violent people.

LANSER *looks at bandage and says nothing.*

HUNTER [*glancing up from board*]: I suggest you start wearing a helmet. [*He looks down at his work again.*]

CORELL [*looks at* HUNTER, *then rises, steps to* LANSER]: I wanted particularly to talk to you, Colonel. I thought I might help with the Civil administration.

LANSER [*walks to the R. end of table—looks at* HUNTER]: What have you in mind?

CORELL: Well, you must have a Mayor you can trust. I thought perhaps Orden might step down now, and . . . Well, if I were to take over his office . . . we could work very nicely together.

LANSER [*his eyes seem to grow large and bright. He turns to* CORELL *and speaks sharply*]: Have you mentioned this in your report to the Capitol?

CORELL: Well, yes . . . naturally, in my analysis . . .

LANSER [*interrupting*]: Have you talked to any of the town people since we arrived—outside the Mayor, that is?

CORELL [*giving ground*]: Well, no. You see, they are still a bit startled. They didn't expect it. [LANSER *crosses to above table, looking at* HUNTER. *Chuckling.*] No, sir, they didn't expect it. [*Sits chair L. of table.*]

LANSER [*pressing his point*]: So you don't really know what is going on in their heads?

CORELL: Why, they've had a shock. They're going to be all right.

LANSER: You don't know what they think of you?

CORELL: I have lots of friends here. I know everyone.

LANSER [*takes a step to him*]: Has anyone bought anything in your store this morning?

CORELL: Naturally, business is at a standstill.

LANSER [*suddenly relaxes. He speaks quietly*]: Yours is a difficult and brave branch of the service. [*Crosses U. to* HUNTER.] It should be greatly rewarded.

CORELL: Thank you, sir.

LANSER: You'll have their hatred in time.

CORELL: I can stand that, sir. They are the enemy.

LANSER [*hesitating a long moment before he speaks. Says almost in a whisper, turning to* CORELL]: You will not even have *our* respect.

CORELL [*jumping to his feet*]: The Leader has said all branches are equally honorable.

LANSER [*still very quietly*]: I hope the Leader is right. I hope he can read the minds of soldiers. [*Crosses to chair R. end table, sits. Pulls himself together.*] Now. We must come to exactness. I am in charge here. I must maintain order and discipline. To do that I must know what is in the minds of these people. I must anticipate revolt.

CORELL [*sits in chair L. of table*]: I can find out what you wish to know, sir. As Mayor here, I will be very effective.

LANSER: Orden is more than Mayor. He *is* the people. He will think what they think. By watching him I will know them. He must stay. That is my judgment.

CORELL: My place is here, sir. I have made my place.

LANSER: I have no orders about this. I must use my own judgment. I think you will never again know what is going on here. I think no one will speak to you. No one will be near to you, except those people who live on money. I think without a bodyguard you will be in great danger. I prefer that you go back to the Capitol.

CORELL: My work, sir, merits better treatment than being sent away.

LANSER [*slowly*]: Yes, it does. But to the larger work I think you are only in the way. If you are not hated yet, you will be. In any little revolt you will be the first to be killed. I suggest that you go back.

CORELL [*rises, stiffly*]: You will, of course, permit me to wait for a reply from the Capitol?

LANSER: Of course. [*Rises.*] But I shall recommend that

you go back for your own safety. Frankly . . . you have no
further value here. [*Crossing.*] But . . . well, there must be
other plans in other countries. Perhaps you will go now to
some new town, win new confidence . . . a greater responsibility. I will recommend you highly for your work here.

CORELL [*his eyes shining with the praise*]: Thank you, sir.
I have worked hard. Perhaps you are right. [*Crosses to
chair above table, puts on coat.*] But I will wait for the
reply from the Capitol.

LANSER [*his voice tight and his eyes slitted. Harshly, crossing to table*]: Wear a helmet. Keep indoors. Do not go out
at night, and above all do not drink. Trust no woman or
any man. You understand?

CORELL [*smiling as though* LANSER *were a petulant child.
Crossing D. to below table*]: I don't think you understand.
I have a little house, a country girl waits on me. I even
think she is fond of me. These are peaceful people.

LANSER: There are no peaceful people. When will you learn
it? There are no friendly people. Can't you understand
that? We have invaded this country. You, by what they
call treachery, prepared for us. [*His face grows red and his
voice rises.*] Can't you understand that we are at war with
these people? [*Crosses U.R.*]

CORELL [*a little smugly*]: We have defeated them.

LANSER [*he goes on as though he were instructing a class.
Crosses to him above table*]: A defeat is a momentary
thing. A defeat doesn't last. We were defeated and now
we are back. Defeat means nothing. Can't you understand
that? Do you know what they are whispering behind
doors?

CORELL: Do you?

The door R. closes suddenly. Both men turn to look.

LANSER: No. [*Crosses to fireplace.*]

CORELL [*crosses quickly to door R., opens it, looks out,*

then closes it and crosses D.R. to LANSER. *Insinuatingly*]:
Are you afraid, Colonel? [LANSER *turns to him.*] Should
our Commander be afraid?

LANSER [*sitting down heavily in arm-chair*]: Maybe that's
it. [*He says disgustedly.*] I am tired of people who have
not been at war who know all about it. [*He is silent for
a moment.*] I remember a little old woman in Brussels.
Sweet face, white hair . . . delicate old hands. [*He seems
to see the figure in front of him.*] She used to sing our
songs to us in a quivering voice. She always knew where
to find a cigarette or a virgin. [LANSER *catches himself as
though he had been asleep.*] We didn't know her son had
been executed. When we finally shot her, she had killed
twelve men with a long black hat-pin.

CORELL [*eagerly*]: But you shot her.

LANSER: Of course we shot her!

CORELL: And the murders stopped?

LANSER: No . . . the murders didn't stop. And when finally
we retreated, the people cut off stragglers. They burned
some. And they gouged the eyes from some. And some
they even crucified.

CORELL: These are not good things to say.

LANSER: They are not good things to remember.

CORELL: You should not be in command if you are afraid.
[*Crosses away from* LANSER *to L. end of table.*]

LANSER [*softly*]: I know how to fight.

CORELL [*turns to him*]: You don't talk this way to the
young officers?

LANSER [*shaking his head*]: No. They wouldn't believe me.

CORELL [*in anger and fear. Crossing toward him*]: Why do
you tell me, then?

LANSER: Because your work is done. Your work is done.

The door U.L. bursts open. CAPTAIN LOFT *enters. He is
rigid and cold and military.*

LOFT: There is trouble, sir.

LANSER [*rises*]: Trouble?

LOFT: Captain Bentick has been hurt.

LANSER: Oh ... yes. [*Crosses to C.* STRETCHER BEAR-
ERS *enter, carrying a figure covered with blankets.* LOFT
crosses to below desk. CORELL *crosses above table.*]
How badly is he hurt?

LOFT [*stiffly*]: I don't know.

PRACKLE *enters from bedroom and stands in doorway.*

LANSER: Put him in there. [*He points to bedroom L. The*
BEARERS *exit L. with their burden.* PRACKLE *exits ahead*
of them. LANSER *follows them off,* HUNTER *crosses to*
front table. CORELL *crosses D.L. After a pause* LANSER
enters, stands at door.] Who killed him?

LOFT: A miner.

HUNTER *crosses back to his drawing-board.*

LANSER: Why?

LOFT: I was there, sir.

LANSER: Well, make your report, then. Make your report,
dammit!

LOFT [*draws himself up and says formally*]: I had just
relieved Captain Bentick as the Colonel ordered. Captain Bentick was about to leave to come here, when I had
some trouble with a miner. He wanted to quit. When I
ordered him to work, he rushes at me with his pick. Captain Bentick tried to interfere.

CORELL *crosses to chair for hat, then exits U.L.* LOFT
turns to watch CORELL.

LANSER [*crosses to C. Sternly*]: You captured the man?

LOFT: Yes, sir.

LANSER [*slowly crossing to fireplace, speaks as though to*
himself]: So it starts again. We'll shoot this man and make

twenty new enemies. It's the only thing we know. The only thing we know.

LOFT [*crossing in to C.*]: What did you say, sir?

LANSER: Nothing. Nothing at all, I was just thinking. [*He turns to* LOFT.] Please give my compliments to Mayor Orden and my request that he see me at once.

LOFT *turns, exits U.L.* HUNTER, *looking up, dries his inking pen carefully and puts it away in its velvet-lined box.*

CURTAIN

PART ONE: SCENE III

SCENE: *The same. Two days later. The disintegration of the room is under way. There is some military equipment about, but a desolateness is apparent from the arrangement of the furniture. The console table U.R. and the large painting above it have gone. The mantel is bare of dressing. The table used in Scene II has been removed. There are newspapers on the floor around the fireplace. Even the grandfather clock has been moved out. Only the* MAYOR'S *desk, chair and the arm-chair R. remain as we first saw them. Five chairs are pushed back against wall U.C., leaving the center of the room quite bare. Three small chairs are D.L. The light is rather cold.* AT RISE: *Curtain rises on an empty stage, but immediately the door R. is opened by* JOSEPH, *who at once turns his back and begins the manoeuvering of a large dining-room table through the door. He talks to* ANNIE *off-stage, who is helping with the other end of the table. The table is so large that it has been turned on its side to get it through the door at all.*

JOSEPH [*edging the legs through door*]: Don't push now, Annie. [*Clears the legs.*] Now push, Annie. Now—
ANNIE [*appears in door at other end of table*]: I am.
JOSEPH: Don't scuff the bottom. Lift—lift on it. Steady!
ANNIE [*a little angrily*]: I am steady.

They manoeuver the table through the door and stand it on its legs. It is quite heavy.

JOSEPH: Now— right over here. Right in the center. [*They put table in C. of room.*] There!

ANNIE [*truculently, as they open table for the leaves*]: If His Excellency hadn't told me to do it I wouldn't. What's a dining table want in here!

JOSEPH [*gets leaves from U.C., takes them to table*]: The Colonel wants it here. They're going to hold some kind of a trial.

ANNIE: Why don't they hold it down at the City Hall where it belongs?

JOSEPH: I don't know. They do crazy things. It's some kind of way they have. [*They close table.*] Look at this room. There's no way to fix it up with their stuff all over. [*Places 2 chairs from U.C. above table.*]

ANNIE [*as though she really doesn't want to know; crossing D.L. for a chair*]: What do they want to have a trial for?

JOSEPH: Well—there's talk. People say there was trouble at the mine. Some kind of a fight.

ANNIE [*her interest is aroused as she crosses to front table with chair*]: You mean they're going to try one of *us*?

JOSEPH: That's what they say. [*Places chair from U.C. at R. end table.*]

ANNIE: Who?

JOSEPH [*places chair from U.C. above table*]: Well, they say Alex Morden got in some kind of trouble at the mine.

ANNIE [*crossing D.L. for 2 chairs*]: That's Molly's husband. He never gets in any trouble. He's a good man. What kind of trouble could Alex get into?

JOSEPH: Well, some people say he hit a soldier. [*Places chair from U.C. at L. end table.*]

ANNIE [*crossing to front table with 2 chairs*]: It's a time of trouble. Molly Kenderly wouldn't have married a man who hit people. Alex is a good man. The soldiers must have done something to Alex. [*Crosses to fireplace.*]

JOSEPH [*crossing C.*]: I don't know. Nobody seems to know what happened. I heard—[*Tiptoes to door L., opens it slowly, then closes it, crosses R. to* ANNIE.]—that William Deal and his wife got away last night in a little boat and I heard that somebody hit that man Corell with a rock. Everybody's uneasy.

ANNIE [*picking up papers at fireplace and sweeping up*]: Uneasy. You should see my sister. Her boy Robbie got away when they killed the other soldiers. Christine thinks she knows where he'd go back in the hills, but she can't find out if he was hurt or anything. She's going crazy worrying. She even wanted me to ask His Excellency to try to find out. He might be hurt. I can't ask His Excellency.

JOSEPH: I know. [MAYOR *enters U.L., standing in doorway, hears himself mentioned and stops.*] People in the town are worried about His Excellency. They don't know where he stands—soldiers in his house and he hasn't said anything. [MAYOR *crosses in to L. end table.*] And you know—everybody liked Corell and then he was for the soldiers. [WINTER *enters U.L. and stands in doorway.*] People are worried about His Excellency.

MAYOR [*looking at table*]: This is right. I guess this is what they want. [*Crosses to desk.* JOSEPH *and* ANNIE *are caught talking about him. They are embarrassed.*] You can tell anyone you see that I haven't gone over to the enemy. I am still the Mayor.

WINTER *crosses U.C. to windows.*

JOSEPH [*crossing C.*]: We didn't mean—

ANNIE [*crossing L. to* MAYOR]: Your Excellency—Christine's boy got away. She thinks he's in the hills and maybe hurt.

MAYOR: Does she know where he is?

ANNIE: She thinks so. About fifteen miles away in the hills.

MAYOR [*turns to* JOSEPH]: Would you go?

JOSEPH: Yes, sir.

MAYOR: Then go tonight. And don't let anyone see you go.

JOSEPH: Yes, Your Excellency.

ANNIE: Thank you, Your Excellency. I'll tell Christine.

> JOSEPH *and* ANNIE *exit R. excitedly, and apparently they are going to spread the news.* WINTER *comes silently down and seats himself in one of the chairs above big table.* MAYOR *speaks out of thought.*

MAYOR: I wonder how much longer I can stay in this position? Which is better—to be thrown out of control or to remain and have the people suspect me?

WINTER: Maybe you could keep control and be with the people, too.

MAYOR: I don't know. The people don't quite trust me and neither does the enemy.

WINTER: You trust yourself, don't you? There is no doubt in your mind where you stand?

MAYOR: Doubt? No, I'm the Mayor. [*Rises, crosses to L. end table.*] I don't understand many things. [*He points to table.*] I don't know why they have to bring this trial in here. They are going to try Alex Morden here for murder. You know Alex. He has that pretty wife, Molly.

WINTER: I remember. She taught in a grammar school before she was married. Yes, I remember her. She was so pretty she hated to get glasses when she needed them. Well, I guess Alex killed an officer all right. Nobody has questioned that.

MAYOR [*bitterly, as he sits chair L. of table*]: Of course, no one questions it. But why do they try him? Why don't they shoot him? We don't try them for killing our soldiers. A trial implies right or wrong, doubt or certainty. There

is none of that here. Why must they try him—and in my
house?

WINTER: I would guess it is for the show. There is an idea
about that if you go through the form of a thing you have
it. They'll have a trial and hope to convince the people
that there is justice involved. Alex did kill the Captain.

MAYOR: Yes, I know.

WINTER: And if it comes from your house, where the people
have always expected justice . . .

*He is interrupted by the door opening R. A young woman
enters. She is about thirty, and quite pretty. She is dressed
simply, neatly. She is excited. This is* MOLLY MORDEN.

MOLLY [*quickly, crossing in to R. end table*]: Annie told me
just to come right in, sir.

MAYOR [*rises, looks at her*]: Why, of course.

MOLLY: They say Alex will be tried and . . . shot. They say
you will try him.

MAYOR [*looks up quickly at* WINTER]: Who says this?

MOLLY [*crossing C.*]: The people in the town. [*She holds
herself very straight. Her voice is half-pleading and
half-demanding.*] You wouldn't do that, would you, sir?

MAYOR [*crossing L. to desk chair*]: How could the people
know what I don't know about myself?

WINTER [*quietly*]: That's a mystery . . . how the people
know. How the truth of things gets out.

MOLLY [*coming near to him*]: Alex is not a murdering man.
He is a quick-tempered man. He has never broken the
law. He is a respected man.

WINTER *crosses to R. end of table.*

MAYOR [*crossing to her*]: I know. [*He is silent for a moment.*]
I've known Alex since he was a little boy. I knew his father
and his grandfather. His grandfather was a bear hunter in
the old days. Did you know that?

MOLLY [*ignores his words*]: You won't sentence Alex?

MAYOR: No. How could I sentence him?

MOLLY [*turns away from him*]: The people said you would for the sake of order.

MAYOR [*a step to her*]: Do the people want order, Molly?

MOLLY [*turns to him*]: They want to be free.

MAYOR: Do they know how to go about it? Do they know what methods to use against this armed enemy?

MOLLY [*her chin comes up*]: No, sir. But I think the people want to show these soldiers that they aren't beaten.

WINTER [*crossing to fireplace*]: They've had no chance to fight. [MOLLY *looks at* WINTER.] It's no fight to go against machine guns.

MAYOR [*crosses to her, takes her hand. She turns to him*]: When you know what the people want to do, will you tell me, Molly?

MOLLY [*looks at him suspiciously, takes away her hand, turns and moves away from him*]: Yes. [*Unconvincingly.*]

MAYOR: You mean no. You don't trust me.

MOLLY [*defiantly, turns to him*]: How about Alex?

MAYOR: I will not sentence him. He has committed no crime against our people.

MOLLY [*fearfully*]: Will they . . . kill Alex? [*Looks at* WINTER. *He crosses to arm-chair, sits. She turns to* MAYOR.]

MAYOR [*stares blankly at her for a moment*]: Dear child, my poor child!

MOLLY [*she stands rigidly, her face very tight*]: Thank you. [MAYOR *comes near her.*] Don't touch me. Please don't touch me. [*Crosses U.L. As she reaches door, she runs out.*] Please don't touch me! [MAYOR *turns as though to follow her.*]

WINTER: Let her go.

MAYOR *stops.* MADAME *comes in door R.*

MADAME [*crossing C. front table*]: I don't know how I can

run the house. It's more people than the house can stand. Annie's angry all the time.

MAYOR [*turns to her*]: Sara—listen to me.

MADAME [*in amazement*]: I don't know what I'm going to do with Annie.

MAYOR: Hush! Sara, I want you to go to Alex Morden's house. You know where it is. Do you understand? I want you to stay with Molly . . . while she needs you. Don't talk; just stay with her.

MADAME: I have a hundred things—

MAYOR [*a little angry*]: I can't understand you. They are going to kill Alex. [*Crosses to chair R. front table, sits.*] I can't see how you can rattle on—the house—the servants—

MADAME [*turns and looks at him with affection. For a moment a mask seems to drop. When she speaks it is in a kind of self-revelation that only comes in great emotion*]: Dear—I am doing what I can. There must be some to do the regular daily thing. When there is a funeral some people mourn and then there are some women in the kitchen cooking. Do you think they feel death less or do you think they know that life goes on in death, that life balances death?

MAYOR [*in wonder, looks up at her*]: And you do know what you are doing. [*In understanding, takes her hand.*] My dear—my very dear—

MADAME: I will go to Molly now. I won't leave her. [*Straightens his hair.*] You need never worry about me. Whether my way is good or not—[*Crossing R.*]—it is my way.

MAYOR [*rises, catches her hand as she passes him*]: Thank you, my dear, for telling me. [*He holds her for a moment, then kisses her on the cheek.*]

MADAME [*looking down, touches a button on his coat*]: You're going to lose this button. I'll sew it back tonight. [*Exits R., closes door.*]

MAYOR [*turns toward door U.L., then back to* WINTER]:
Doctor, how do you think Molly looked?

WINTER: She'll be all right. Close to hysteria, I guess. But
she's good stock. Good strong stock. She'll be all right.

LANSER [*comes in stiffly U.L. He has on a new pressed
uniform with a little dagger at the belt*]: Your Excellency.
[*He glances at* WINTER.] Doctor. I'd like to speak to you
alone.

MAYOR: Doctor!

LANSER *crosses U.R. above table.*

WINTER [*rises, crosses L. front of table*]: Yes.

MAYOR: Will you come back to me this evening?

WINTER: Well, I have a patient—

MAYOR: I have a feeling I'll want you here with me.

WINTER: I'll be here. [*Crosses to doors U.L.*] I'll be here.
[*Closes doors after him, exits.*]

LANSER [*waits courteously. Watches door close. He looks
at table and chairs arranged about it, crosses to R. end
table*]: I'm very sorry about this. I wish it hadn't happened. [MAYOR *faces away from* LANSER.] I like you,
and I respect you. I have a job to do. You surely recognize
that. [MAYOR *does not answer. At the end of each sentence* LANSER *waits for an answer, and none comes.*] We
don't act on our own judgment. There are rules laid down
for us. Rules made in the Capitol. This man has killed an
officer.

ORDEN [*slowly turns to him*]: Why didn't you shoot him
then? That was the time to do it.

LANSER [*crossing U.R.*]: Even if I agreed with you, it
would make no difference. You know as well as I that
punishment is for the purpose of preventing other crimes.
[*Crosses to table.*] Since it is for others, punishment must
be publicized. It must even be dramatized. [MAYOR *turns
away to his desk.*]

MAYOR: Yes—I know the theory—I wonder whether it works. [*Sits desk chair.*]

LANSER: Mayor Orden, you know our orders are inexorable. We must get the coal. If your people are not orderly, we will have to restore that order by force. [*His voice grows stern.*] We must shoot people if it is necessary. If you wish to save your people from hurt, you will help us to keep order. Now . . . [*Crossing to above table.*] . . . it is considered wise by my government that punishments emanate from the local authorities.

MAYOR [*softly, rises, crosses to chair L. of table*]: So . . . the people did know, they do know—[*Speaks louder.*] You wish me to pass sentence of death on Alexander Morden after a trial here?

LANSER: Yes. And you will prevent a great deal of bloodshed later if you will do it.

MAYOR [*pulls out the chair at L. end and sits down. He seems to be the judge and* LANSER *the culprit. He drums his fingers on table*]: You and your government do not understand. In all the world yours is the only government and people with a record of defeat after defeat for centuries, and always because you did not understand. [*He pauses for a moment.*] This principle does not work. First, I am the Mayor. I have no right to pass sentence of death under our law. There is no one in this community with that right. If I should do it I would be breaking the law as much as you.

LANSER: Breaking the law?

MAYOR: You killed six men when you came in and you hurt others. Under our law you were guilty of murder, all of you. Why do you go into this nonsense of law, Colonel? There is no law between you and us. This is war. You destroyed the law when you came in, and a new cruel law took its place. You know you'll have to kill all of us or we in time will kill all of you.

LANSER: May I sit down?

MAYOR: Why do you ask? That's another lie. You could make *me* stand if you wanted.

LANSER [*seats himself R. end table*]: No . . . I respect you and your office, but what I think—I, a man of certain age and certain memories—is of no importance. I might agree with you, but that would change nothing. The military, the political pattern I work in, has certain tendencies and practices which are invariable.

MAYOR: And these tendencies and practices have been proven wrong in every single test since the beginning of the world.

LANSER [*laughing bitterly*]: I, a private man—with certain memories—might agree with you. Might even add that one of the tendencies of the military mind is an inability to learn. An inability to see beyond the killing which is its job. [*He straightens his shoulders.*] But I am not a private man. The coal miner must be shot . . . publicly, because the theory is that others will then restrain themselves from killing our men.

MAYOR: Then we needn't talk any more.

LANSER: Yes, we must talk. We want you to help.

MAYOR [*sits quietly for a moment, then looks up smiling*]: I'll tell you what I'll do. How many men were on the machine guns that killed our soldiers?

LANSER: About twenty.

MAYOR: Very well. If you will shoot them, I will usurp the power to condemn Morden.

LANSER: You are not serious?

MAYOR: I am serious.

LANSER: This can't be done, you know it. This is nonsense.

MAYOR: I know it. And what you ask can't be done. It is nonsense too.

LANSER [*sighing*]: I suppose I knew it. Maybe Corell will

have to be Mayor after all. [*He looks up quickly.*] You'll
stay for the trial?

MAYOR [*with warmth*]: Yes, I'll stay. Then he won't be
alone.

LANSER [*looks at him and smiles sadly*]: We've taken on a
job, haven't we?

MAYOR: Yes. The one impossible job in the world. The one
thing that can't be done.

LANSER: Yes?

MAYOR: To break man's spirit . . . permanently. [MAYOR'S
*head sinks a little toward table. The room is quite dark
by now.*]

A SLOW CURTAIN

PART ONE: SCENE IV

SCENE: *It is a half hour later.*

The same as before. The room is fairly dark. The brackets in the little drawing-room are lighted. The room has been stripped of all its pictures, bric-a-brac and furniture, except the long dining-room table which is in the center, and 5 chairs around the table. 3 small chairs are standing against wall L. On the wall L. above where the MAYOR'S *desk stood, an iron bracket has been driven into the wall and a lighted gasoline lantern hangs. The court martial is in session.*

LANSER *sits above table C., with* HUNTER *on his R.* TONDER *stands at attention U.R.* LOFT, *with a little pile of papers in front of him, sits R. end table.* MAYOR *sits on* LANSER'S *L., and* PRACKLE *is at L. end table.* PRACKLE *is doodling with his pencil. Guarding the doors U.L. and facing the audience, two* GUARDS *stand with bayonets fixed, with helmets on their heads. Another* SOLDIER *stands at door D.L. They are wooden images. And between them stands* ALEX MORDEN, *a big young man with a wide, low forehead, deep-set eyes and a long sharp nose. His chin is firm, his mouth sensual and wide. He is a big man, broad of shoulder and narrow of hip. In front of him his manacled hands clasp and unclasp, and make a little clink of metal. He is dressed in black trousers, a blue shirt, a dark blue tie, and a dark coat shiny with wear.* LOFT *is*

standing at his end of table, beginning to read from a paper.
He reads mechanically.

LOFT: "When ordered back to work, he refused to go. And
when the order was repeated, the prisoner attacked Captain Loft with a pickaxe. Captain Bentick interposed his
body . . ."

MAYOR: Sit down, Alex. [LOFT *stops reading and glances*
at him.] One of you guards get him a chair.

One of the GUARDS *turns and hauls up a chair unques-*
tioningly from wall L. to L.C.

LOFT: It is customary for the prisoner to stand.

MAYOR: Let him sit down. Only we will know. You can
report that he stood.

LOFT [*stiffly*]: It is not customary to falsify reports.

MAYOR: Sit down, Alex. [ALEX *sits down and his manacled*
hands are restless.]

LOFT: This is contrary to all . . .

LANSER [*looks up from writing, interrupting*]: Let him sit
down.

LOFT [*clears throat and continues to read*]: "Captain Bentick
interposed his body and received a blow on the head
which crushed his skull." A medical report is appended.
Does the Colonel wish me to read it?

LANSER: No need. Make it as short as you can.

LOFT [*reading*]: "These facts have been witnessed by several of our soldiers, whose statements are attached. This
military court finds the prisoner guilty of murder and rec-
ommends the death sentence." Does the Colonel wish me
to read the statements of the soldiers?

LANSER [*sighing*]: No. [LOFT *sits.* LANSER *turns to* ALEX.]
You don't deny you killed the Captain, do you?

ALEX [*smiling sadly*]: I hit him. I don't know that I killed
him. I didn't see him afterwards.

MAYOR *and* ALEX *smile at each other.*

LOFT [*rising*]: Does the prisoner mean to imply that Captain Bentick was killed by someone else?

ALEX: I don't know. I only hit him . . . and then somebody hit me.

LANSER [*wearily*]: Do you want to offer any explanation? I can't think of anything that will change the sentence, but we'll listen.

LOFT [*breaking in*]: I respectfully submit that the Colonel should not have said that. It indicates that the court is not impartial. [*Sits.*]

LANSER [*looks at* MAYOR, *then says to* ALEX]: Have you any explanation?

ALEX [*lifts right hand to gesture, and the manacle brings the left hand with it. He looks embarrassed and puts them into his lap again*]: I was mad, I guess. I have a pretty bad temper and when he said I had to go to work . . . I got mad and I hit him. I guess I hit him hard. It was the wrong man. [*He points at* LOFT.] That is the man I wanted to hit. That one.

LANSER: It doesn't matter who you wanted to hit. Anybody would have been the same. Are you sorry you did it? It would look well in the record if he were sorry.

Speaks aside to LOFT *and* HUNTER.

ALEX [*puzzled*]: Sorry? I'm not sorry. He told me to go to work. I'm a free man. I used to be Alderman. He said I had to work.

LANSER: But if the sentence is death, won't you be sorry then?

ALEX [*sinks his head and ponders honestly*]: No. You mean would I do it again?

LANSER: That's what I mean.

ALEX [*thoughtfully*]: I do not think I'm sorry.

LANSER: Put in the record that the prisoner is overcome with remorse. Sentence is automatic, you understand. The court has no leeway. The court finds you guilty and sentences you to be shot immediately. I do not see any reason to torture you with this any more. Now, is there anything I have forgotten?

MAYOR: You have forgotten me. [*He stands up, pushes back his chair and steps over to* ALEX.] Alexander, I am the Mayor . . . elected.

ALEX: I know it, sir. [*Starts to stand, but* MAYOR, *hand on his shoulder, eases* ALEX *back into chair.*]

MAYOR: Alex, these men have taken our country by treachery and force.

LOFT [*rising*]: Sir, this should not be permitted.

LANSER [*rising*]: Be silent. Is it better to hear it, or would you rather it were whispered? [*Crosses U. to windows.*]

MAYOR [*continuing*]: When the enemy came, the people were confused and I was confused. Yours was the first clear act. Your private anger was the beginning of a public anger. I know it is said in the town that I am acting with these men. I will show the town that I am not. . . . But you . . . you are going to die. [*Softly.*] I want you to know.

ALEX [*dropping his head and then raising it*]: I know it. I know it, sir.

LANSER [*loudly, crossing to* LOFT]: Is the squad ready?

LOFT [*rising*]: Outside, sir.

LANSER: Who is commanding? [*Crossing to fireplace.*]

LOFT: Lieutenant Tonder, sir. [TONDER *raises his head, and his chin is hard but his eyes are frightened.* LANSER *looks at his watch.*]

MAYOR [*softly*]: Are you afraid, Alex?

ALEX: Yes, sir.

MAYOR: I can't tell you not to be. I would be, too. And so would these . . . young gods of war.

LANSER [*facing table*]: Call your squad. [OFFICERS *at the table rise, stand at attention.*]

TONDER [*crossing to* LANSER]: They're here, sir. [*Crosses L. to doors U.L., then* TWO SOLDIERS *step to* ALEX.]

MAYOR: Alex, go knowing that these men will have no rest . . . no rest at all until they are gone . . . or dead. You will make the people one. It's little enough gift to you, but it is so. . . . No rest at all. [ALEX *has shut his eyes tightly.* MAYOR *leans close and kisses him on the cheek.*] Goodbye, Alex. [*The* GUARDS *take* ALEX *by the arm and guide him. He keeps his eyes tightly closed. They guide him through the door between them. The* THIRD SOLDIER *and* TONDER *follow them out. The sound of the squad's feet in the passageway marches on wood and out of the house. The* MEN *about the table are silent. Outside the snow begins to fall.*] I hope you know what you are doing.

LOFT *gathers his papers together. From outside come the commands* "Attention! Right Face! Forward March!" *and the* SOLDIERS' *footsteps are heard disappearing.*

LANSER: In the Square, Captain?

LOFT: In the Square. It must be public.

MAYOR: I hope you know what you are doing.

LANSER: Man, whether we know it or not, it is what must be done.

A silence falls on the room and each man listens. After ten seconds, from the distance comes the commands. "Ready! Aim! Fire!", followed by the blast of a machine gun. MAYOR puts his hands to his forehead and fills his lungs deeply. LOFT and HUNTER sit at their places. LANSER crosses U. to his chair. As he reaches it, suddenly there is a shot outside. The glass of the window crashes inward. PRACKLE wheels about. He puts his hand to his shoulder.

HUNTER *and* LOFT *jump away from table and draw their revolvers.*

LANSER [*sharply*]: Rigid! [OFFICERS *snap to attention;* LANSER, *to* PRACKLE.] Are you badly hurt?

PRACKLE: My shoulder.

LANSER [*crossing D. to table*]: Report to the hospital!

PRACKLE: Sir! [*Picks up helmet and coat, exits U.L.*]

LANSER: Captain Loft!

LOFT: Sir!

LANSER: Find the man who fired that shot.

LOFT: Sir! [*Picks up helmet and coat, exits U.L., running.*]

LANSER *to* LOFT [*as he goes*]: There should be tracks in the snow. [*From outside the commands*: "Company attention! Left face! Double quick forward march!", *and the sound of running soldiers.*] Major Hunter, take Lieutenant Tonder and a detail. Search every house in the town for weapons. Shoot down any resistance. Take five hostages for execution.

HUNTER: Sir! [*Picks up helmet and coat, exits U.L.*]

LANSER: You, Mayor Orden, are in protective custody.

MAYOR: A man of certain memories.

LANSER: A man of no memories. We will shoot five—ten—a hundred for one! [*Crosses to window, then to L. end table.*] So it starts again.

MAYOR [*crossing to R. end table*]: It's beginning to snow.

LANSER: We'll have to have that glass fixed. The wind blows cold through a broken window.

MAYOR: Yes, the wind blows cold!

CURTAIN

PART TWO

PART TWO: SCENE I

TIME: *Two months later.*

SCENE: *Still the downstairs room. It will be even more changed now. A kind of discomfort will have crept in. A slight mess due not to dirt so much as to the business of the men. It is very cold outside and not comfortably warm inside. Let the men wear coats and seem to be a little chilly all the time. This scene takes place at night. The blackout curtains are drawn tight. On the table, the same dining-room table, there are two gasoline lanterns which throw a hard white light.* [NOTE: *These lanterns have to be pumped occasionally to keep the pressure up.*] *The light is cold and throws hard shadows. Also such a light from below will distort faces by throwing the light upward. On the table are several tin cups and plates. The room has been stripped bare of all drapes. Over the mantel hangs a map of the locality. Against the wall R. is a stack of duffle bags filled with equipment. More duffle-bags stand against the wall U.R. On this wall hangs a work drawing of* HUNTER'S *rail line from the mine to the dock. A surveyor's sight on a tripod stands in a corner. At the windows U.C. on the table that was there in Scene I stands a Maxim machine gun pointing out the L. window. The cartridge belt is in place. Sandbags support the gun. On the wall U.L. hangs a bulletin board with a mail box. Against the L. wall where the* MAYOR'S *desk stood there now is an army cot with pillow*

*and blankets. On this wall upstage is a board with nails from
which hang a Tommy gun, a duffle-bag, several greatcoats
and helmets. Downstage on the wall hangs another work
drawing. From this wall, also, hangs a newspaper-shaded
lamp.*

Throughout the scene the sound of wind outside is heard.
AT RISE: HUNTER *is sitting at his drawing board at L.
end table, working with T-square and triangle.* PRACKLE
*sits in a straight chair, his feet up on another, in front of a
stove that has been set up front of the mantel, reading an
illustrated paper. Behind the table* TONDER *is writing a
letter. He holds the pen pinched high, and occasionally
looks up from his letter; looks at the ceiling as though
thinking, then nervously crumples the paper he has been
writing on, throws it away and starts his letter again.*

PRACKLE [*looking down at illustrated paper*]: I can close
   my eyes and see every shop on this street here. [HUNTER
   goes on with his work and TONDER *writes a few words.*]
   There is a restaurant right behind here. You can't see it in
   the picture, called Burden's.
HUNTER [*without looking up*]: I know the place. They had
   good pastry.
PRACKLE: Do you remember those little poppyseed cakes?
   Everything was good there. Not a single bad thing did
   they serve, and their coffee . . .
TONDER: They won't be serving coffee now—or cakes.
PRACKLE: Well, I don't know about that. They did and they
   will again, and there was a waitress there— [*He looks
   down at magazine.*] She had the strangest eyes—has, I
   mean—always kind of moist-looking as though she had
   just been laughing or crying. [*He looks at ceiling and
   speaks softly.*] I was out with her. She was something. I
   wonder why I didn't go back oftener. I wonder if she is
   still there.

TONDER [*gloomily*]: Probably not. Working in a factory, maybe.

PRACKLE [*laughing*]: I hope they aren't rationing girls at home.

TONDER: It'll probably come to that, too.

PRACKLE [*playfully turning to him*]: You don't care much for girls, do you? Not much you don't!

TONDER [*puts down his pen*]: I like them for what girls are for. I don't let them crawl around my other life.

PRACKLE [*tauntingly turns back to his magazine*]: Seems to me they crawl all over you all the time.

TONDER [*obviously to change the subject. Rises, pumps lantern on R. end table*]: I hate these damn lanterns. Major, when are you going to get that dynamo fixed?

HUNTER: Should be done by now. I have plenty of good men working on it and I'll double the guard on it from now on. [TONDER *crosses to lantern L. and pumps it.*]

PRACKLE: Did you get the fellow that wrecked it?

HUNTER [*a little grimly*]: Might be any one of five men. I got all five! [TONDER *crosses to his chair, sits. Musingly.*] It's so damn easy to wreck a dynamo if you know how. Just short it and it wrecks itself. The light ought to be on any time now.

PRACKLE [*still looking at magazine*]: I wonder when we'll be relieved? I wonder when we can go home for awhile? [*Looking at him.*] Major, wouldn't you like to go home for a while?

HUNTER [*looks up from his work and his face is hopeless for a moment*]: Yes. Of course. [*He recovers himself.*] I've re-built this four times. [*He indicates drawing-board.*] I don't know why the bombs always choose this particular siding. I'm getting tired of this piece of track. Can't fill in the craters. The ground is frozen too hard.

The electric lights come on. TONDER *reaches out and*

turns off gasoline lantern on table R. HUNTER *turns off lantern near him.*

TONDER: Thank God for that. These lights make me nervous. They're cold. [*He folds the letter he has been writing.*] I wonder why more letters don't come through? I've only had one in three weeks.

PRACKLE: Maybe she doesn't write to you.

TONDER: Maybe. [*He is nervous. Says to* HUNTER.] If anything happened—at home, I mean—do you think they'd let us know? Anything bad, I mean? Any deaths or things like that?

There is a light tap on door R. and JOSEPH *comes in with a scuttle of coal. He moves silently through the room and sets scuttle down at stove so softly it makes no noise. He turns, without looking at anyone, and goes silently toward door.*

PRACKLE [*loudly*]: Joseph! [JOSEPH *turns without replying and without looking up, and bows very slightly.*] Joseph, is there any wine, any brandy? [JOSEPH *shakes his head.*]

TONDER [*starts, his face wild with anger. Shouts*]: Answer, you swine! Answer in words!

JOSEPH [*does not look up; speaks tonelessly*]: No, sir. No, sir, there is no wine.

TONDER [*furiously*]: And no brandy?

JOSEPH [*looking down, speaks tonelessly again*]: There is no brandy, sir. [*He stands perfectly still.*]

TONDER *crosses to mail-box, seals envelope, drops letter, turns back to his chair and sees* JOSEPH *still standing.*

TONDER: What do you want?

JOSEPH: I want to go, sir.

TONDER [*furiously*]: Then go, God damn it!

JOSEPH *turns and is about to leave the room.*

HUNTER: Wait a minute. Is there some coffee?

JOSEPH [*pausing*]: Yes, sir.

HUNTER: Well, bring a pot of coffee. [JOSEPH *exits.*]

HUNTER [*looks at* TONDER]: He had you shouting. That's what he wanted to do.

TONDER [*shakily*]: I'm all right. Sometimes they drive me a little crazy. You know they're always listening behind doors—[*Softly.*] I'd like to get out of this Godforsaken hole!

PRACKLE [*bitterly*]: Tonder was going to live here after the war. [*He imitates* TONDER'S *voice.*] "Put four or five farms together. Make a nice place—kind of a family seat," wasn't it? Going to be a little Lord of the Valley, weren't you? "Nice, pleasant people—beautiful lawns and deer and little children." Isn't that the way it was, Tonder?

TONDER [*as he speaks* TONDER'S *head drops and he clasps his temples with his hands and speaks with emotion*]: Don't talk like that. These horrible people! They're cold! They never look at you, never speak. They answer like dead men. They obey. And the girls frozen—frozen.

JOSEPH *enters with a large coffee-pot.*

HUNTER: Put it down there. [*He puts it on table.*] That's all. [JOSEPH *exits silently.* PRACKLE *crosses to table, pours cup of coffee and takes it to* HUNTER.] Thanks.

TONDER *pours himself cup of coffee.* PRACKLE *crosses back and pours one for himself.*

TONDER [*tastes coffee, licks his lips*]: Does it taste all right to you?

HUNTER [*tasting*]: It isn't very good.

TONDER: But it's kind of bitter—not like coffee.

PRACKLE *tastes his.* HUNTER *takes another drink.*

HUNTER [*sharply*]: Now let's stop this nonsense. The coffee is good or it isn't. If it is good, drink it. If it isn't, don't drink it. [*Puts down his cup.*] Let's not have this questioning.

PRACKLE [*attempting to be light*]: I heard a funny thing the other day. Sergeant Mars told me he heard that a whole company in the South died from mushroom poisoning put in a stew. Five of my men got stomachaches right away.

TONDER [*puts down his cup*]: We shouldn't let them handle anything we eat. They could put poison in everything.

HUNTER: You're just as bad as your men. You halfway believe what you're saying. [*Drinks from his coffee cup.*]

TONDER [*crosses L. to cot bed, sits*]: It's just bad coffee—that's all. Bad, bitter coffee. [*Puts down cup.*]

PRACKLE: I hope so. [*Finishes his coffee. Rises, crosses to his chair D.R. Laughs as though he is saying a silly thing.*] God help us if they ever get top hand! [*Sits.*]

TONDER [*puts hands to his temples. Speaks brokenly*]: There's no rest from it day or night. [*His voice has a soft tenseness of controlled hysteria.*] No rest off duty. [*Breaks for a moment.*] I'd like to go home. I want to talk to a girl. There's a girl in this town. I see her all the time. I want to talk to that girl.

At that moment the lights go out again, leaving the stage in darkness. HUNTER'S *voice speaks while he lights lanterns.*

HUNTER: There they go again. [*Lights lantern L.*] Everybody in town seems to take a crack at my dynamo. [*Crosses to lantern R., lights it.*] You know, the other day a little boy shinnied up a pole and smashed a transformer. [*Crosses to his chair.*] What can you do with children? [*Crosses to* TONDER. *Speaks paternally to him.*] Tonder, do your talking to us, if you have to talk. There's nothing these people would like better than to know that your nerves are getting thin. [*Crosses to his chair, sits.*] Don't let the enemy hear you talk this way.

TONDER: That's it! The enemy—everywhere! Every man and woman. Even children. Waiting. The white faces behind the curtains, listening. We've beaten them. We've won everywhere and they wait and obey and they wait. Half the world is ours. Is it the same in other places, Major?

HUNTER: I don't know. [*Goes back to his work.*]

TONDER: That's it, we don't know. The reports—"everything under control, everything under control." Conquered countries cheer our soldiers. Cheer the New Order. [*His voice changes and grows softer.*] What do the reports say about us? Do they say we're cheered, loved, flowers in our paths?

HUNTER [*as though to a child*]: Now that's off your chest, do you feel better?

TONDER *rises, exits L.*

PRACKLE [*miserably*]: He shouldn't talk that way. Let him keep things to himself. He's a soldier, isn't he? Let him be a soldier.

Door U.L. opens quietly and LOFT *comes in. His nose is pinched and red. His great overcoat collar is high about his ears. He takes off his helmet and gloves, puts them on bed.*

LOFT: I see they got your dynamo again. Your men ought to be more careful.

HUNTER: I heard you had a little trouble at the mine today.

LOFT: Well, I fixed that. [*Taking off his coat.*]

PRACKLE: What happened? [LOFT *turns sharply to him.*] Sir.

LOFT [*hangs his coat on nail U.L.*]: Oh, the usual thing. The slow-down and a wrecked dumpcar. I saw the wrecker, though. Shot him. [*Crossing R.*] I have a cure for it now, though. Each man takes out a certain amount of coal. Can't starve the men or they can't work. But if the coal doesn't come out—[*Crosses to door R., closes it, then crosses to stove.*]—no food for the families. We'll have the men eat at the mine so there's no dividing at home. That will cure it. They work or their kids don't eat. I told them just now.

HUNTER: What did they say?

LOFT [*crossing to R. end table. His eyes narrow fiercely*]: Say? What do they ever say? Nothing. [*Bangs his fist on table.*] Nothing at all! Well, you'll see the coal come out now. [*Turns R. and stops short as he sees that the door he has just closed is open again. Turns to* HUNTER.] I thought I closed that tight.

HUNTER: You did.

LOFT *quietly approaches door, draws his revolver, kicks door wide open and exits. At that moment* TONDER *enters from L., closes door after him.* LOFT *enters from R. and closes door. Crosses to* PRACKLE.

PRACKLE [*turning pages of his illustrated paper again*]: Captain, have you seen these monster guns we were using in the East?

LOFT: Oh, yes. I've seen them fired. They are wonderful.

TONDER [*breaks in, crossing C. to front table*]: Captain, do you get much news from home?

LOFT: Yes—a certain amount.

TONDER: Is everything all right there?

LOFT: Wonderful. We move ahead everywhere.

TONDER: The British aren't defeated yet?

LOFT: They are defeated in every engagement.

TONDER: But they fight on?

LOFT: A few air raids, no more.

TONDER: And the Russians?

LOFT: It's all over.

TONDER [*insistently*]: But they fight on!

LOFT: A little skirmishing.

TONDER: Then we've just about won, Captain?

LOFT [*looks up at him*]: Yes.

TONDER [*looks closely at him*]: You believe this, don't you, Captain?

LOFT [*crossing toward* TONDER]: I don't know what you mean—?

TONDER: We'll be going home before long, then?

LOFT: Well, the reorganization will take a long time. The New Order can't be put into effect in a day.

TONDER: All our lives, perhaps?

HUNTER: Quiet, Tonder!

LOFT [*comes close to* TONDER]: Lieutenant, I don't like the tone of your questions. I don't like the tone of doubt.

TONDER *turns away, crosses U.L.*

HUNTER [*looking up*]: Don't be hard on him, Loft. He's tired. We're all tired.

LOFT: I'm tired, too, but I don't let doubt get in.

HUNTER [*irritably*]: Don't devil him. [LOFT *crosses to above table to pour cup of coffee.*] Where's the Colonel, do you know?

LOFT: Making his report. He's asking for reinforcements. [PRACKLE *and* TONDER *turn to look at him.*] It's a bigger job than we thought.

PRACKLE [*excitedly, rises, crosses to him*]: Will he get them?

LOFT: Of course.

TONDER [*smiles*]: Reinforcements. [*Softly.*] Or maybe

replacements. [*Crossing above table to* LOFT.] Maybe we could go home for awhile. [*He is smiling.*] I could walk down the street and people would say "hello" and they'd like me.

PRACKLE [*crossing D.R.*]: Don't start talking like that. [*Sits.*]

TONDER: There would be friends about and I could turn my back to a man without being afraid.

LOFT [*disgustedly*]: We've enough trouble without having the staff go crazy.

TONDER [*insistently*]: You really think replacements will come, Captain?

LOFT: Certainly. Look, Lieutenant, we've conquered half the world. We must police it for awhile.

TONDER: But the other half?

LOFT: It will fight on hopelessly for awhile.

TONDER: Then we must be spread out all over?

LOFT: For awhile.

TONDER [*breaking over*]: Maybe it will never be over. Maybe it can't be over. Maybe we've made some horrible mistake.

HUNTER: Shut up, Tonder!

LOFT [*rises. During this speech he has drawn himself up until he is a hard rigid thing, his jaw set and tight, his eyes squinted with intensity*]: Lieutenant—if you had said this outside this room, I should prefer a charge of treason against you. Treason not only against the Leader but against your race. Perhaps you are tired. That is no excuse. We are all tired, but we do not forget the destiny of our race. Make no mistake, Lieutenant, we shall conquer the world. We shall impose our faith and our strength on the world. And any weakness in ourselves we shall cut off. I will not bring the charge this time. But I will be watching you. Weakness is treason—do not forget it. [*Crosses L. to cot bed.*]

TONDER [*looking up at him*]: Weakness?

LOFT [*as he sits*]: Weakness is treason!

TONDER: Weakness is treason? [*Sits in his chair above table.*]

PRACKLE [*nervously*]: Stop it! [*Rises, crosses to above stove. To* HUNTER.] Make him stop it!

TONDER [*to himself*]: Treason?

HUNTER: Be quiet, Tonder!

TONDER [*he speaks like a man a little out of his head. Laughingly, a little embarrassedly as he speaks*]: I had a funny dream. I guess a dream. Maybe it was a thought. Or a dream. [*Leans back in his chair.*]

PRACKLE: Stop it.

TONDER: Captain, is this place conquered?

LOFT: Of course.

TONDER [*a little note of hysteria creeps into his laugh*]: Conquered, and we are afraid. Conquered, and we are surrounded. I had a dream. Out in the snow with the black shadows. And the cold faces in doorways. I had a thought. Or a dream.

LOFT *rises.*

PRACKLE: Stop it!

TONDER: I dreamed the Leader was crazy.

HUNTER *laughs and is joined in the laughter by* LOFT *and* PRACKLE.

HUNTER [*turns to* LOFT, *trying to make a joke of it*]: The Leader crazy!

LOFT: Crazy! The enemy have found out how crazy!

The laughter grows to a peak.

TONDER [*who has not stopped laughing*]: Conquest after conquest! [HUNTER *stops laughing, then* LOFT *and* PRACKLE *stop.*] Deeper and deeper into molasses. Maybe

the Leader's crazy. Flies conquer the fly-paper. Flies cap-
ture two hundred miles of new fly-paper. [*His laughter is
hysterical now.*]

LOFT [*gradually realizing the laughter is hysterical. He steps
close to* TONDER, *pulls him up out of his chair and slaps
him in the face*]: Lieutenant! Stop it! Stop it!

TONDER [*the laughter stops. The stage is quiet.* TONDER
*in amazement feels his bruised face with his hand. He
looks at his hand for a moment, sits in his chair, sobbing*]:
I want to go home. [*His head sinks down on the table.*]

CURTAIN

PART TWO: SCENE II

TIME: *Evening of the next day.*

SCENE: *The living-room of* MOLLY MORDEN'S *house. A pleasant, small room, rather poor and very comfortable. An arch R. leads to the kitchen. Downstage of this entrance stands an iron stove. On the floor beside it are a coal bucket, shovel, poker, a wood basket, and papers. Front of the stove is a straight chair facing into the room. Upstage of the kitchen entrance is another straight chair, and in the corner above this is a tall corner cabinet. Against the wall opposite the stove is an armless settee and a square table on which stands a brass oil lamp with a glass shade. Sewing-basket and materials, woolen cloth and a long scissors. The door to the passageway that leads to the outside is to the L. of settee. In the wall L. of this door is a window covered with blackout curtains. House plants stand on the window ledge. Under the window is a large chest. Rugs are on the floor. On shelves above the door L. and entrance R., and on the corner cabinet, stand a variety of decorative plates, pewter and copper utensils. The walls are papered in a warm blue with an old-fashioned fleur de lys design. On the walls are pictures. The light in the room is warm and soft.*

MOLLY MORDEN *is sitting alone on the settee beside the table. She is cutting the woolen material with the scissors. She is pretty and young and neat. Her golden hair is done on the top of her head, tied up with a blue bow. It is a quiet night. The wind whistles a little in the chimney now and then. There is a little rustle at the door and three sharp knocks. She puts down the material, goes to the door and opens it and calls.*

MOLLY: Yes!
ANNIE [*off*]: It's me—Annie.

   MOLLY *goes into storm passage.*

MOLLY: Hello, Annie. I didn't expect you tonight.

A moment later a heavily-cloaked figure enters. This is ANNIE, *the cook, red-nosed, red-eyed and wrapped in non-descript mufflers and a dark cap that covers her head. She slips in quickly as though used to getting speedily through doors and getting them closed behind her. She stands sniffling her red nose and glancing quickly around the room.*

ANNIE: It's cold out, all right. The soldiers brought the winter early. My father always said a war brought bad weather, or bad weather brought a war. [MOLLY *enters, having bolted outside door, and closes door.*] He didn't know which.
MOLLY [*crossing to settee—places scissors on it*]: Take off your things and come to the stove.
ANNIE [*importantly*]: No. I can't wait. *They're* coming!
MOLLY [*crossing to her*]: Who?
ANNIE [*sniffling*]: The Anders boys are sailing for England tonight. They got to. They're hiding now. The Mayor wants to see them before they go.
MOLLY: What happened?
ANNIE: Their brother Jack was shot for wrecking a little dump car. The soldiers are looking for the rest of the family. Know how they do?

MOLLY: Yes, I know how they do.

ANNIE [*crosses to her. Holds out her hand. There is a little package in it*]: Here, take it. I stole it from the Colonel's plate. It's meat.

MOLLY: Thank you, Annie. Did you get some? [*Crosses R.*]

ANNIE: I cook it, don't I? I always get some. [*Crosses to stove, puts coal on fire.*]

MOLLY [*enters, crosses to settee, sits*]: Sit down, Annie, please, and stay awhile.

ANNIE [*crossing to door L.*]: No time. I got to go back and tell the Mayor it's all right here.

MOLLY [*rises, crosses L. to chest*]: It's an awful night to be sailing.

ANNIE: They're fishing men. [*Speaks simply.*] It's better than getting shot.

MOLLY: Yes, so it is. [*Sits on chest.*] How will the Mayor get out?

ANNIE [*laughs*]: Joseph is going to be in his bed in case they look in. Right in his night-shirt. Right next to Madame. [*She laughs again.*] Joseph better lie pretty quiet. [*Exit into hall.*]

MOLLY [*following her off*]: How soon are they coming?

ANNIE [*off*]: Maybe half. Maybe three-quarters of an hour. I'll come in first. Nobody bothers about me. [*She exits.*]

MOLLY *bolts door, comes back into room, crosses to settee, picks up scissors. There is a knocking at outer door.*

MOLLY [*crosses to door, calls*]: Annie! [*Knocking comes again. She goes into passage and we hear her voice.*] What do you want?

MAN'S VOICE: I come to—I don't mean any harm.

MOLLY *enters room, followed by* TONDER. *She tries to close door on him, but he prevents it.*

MOLLY: What do you want? You can't come in here.

TONDER [dressed in his greatcoat]: I don't mean any harm. Please let me come in.

MOLLY [trying to close door on him]: Get out!

TONDER: Miss, I only want to talk. That's all. I want to hear you talk. That's all I want.

MOLLY: I don't want to talk to you!

TONDER: Please, Miss. Just let me stay a little while. Then I'll go. Please. [MOLLY releases door, crosses R. TONDER enters quickly and closes door. Trying to explain.] Just for a little while couldn't we forget the war? Couldn't we talk together? Like people, together? Just for a little while?

MOLLY [turns and looks at him]: You don't know who I am, do you?

TONDER: I've seen you in the town. I know I want to talk to you.

MOLLY [he stands like a child looking very clumsy, as she says very softly]: Why, you are lonely. [Crosses to stove.] It's as simple as that.

TONDER [crossing to settee. Speaks eagerly]: That's it. You understand. I knew you would. [The words come tumbling out of him.] I am lonely to the point of illness. It's nice here. It's warm. Can't I stay, please? [He starts to unbutton his coat, but stops as she continues.]

MOLLY: You can stay for a moment.

He crosses to chest and puts down his helmet. She looks at the stove. The house creaks. He becomes tense.

TONDER [tense]: Is someone here?

MOLLY [crossing to chair front stove]: No. The snow is heavy on the roof. [Sits looking at him.] I have no man any more to push it down.

TONDER [gently]: Did—was it something we did?

MOLLY: Yes.

TONDER: I'm sorry. [*He pauses for a moment.*] I wish I could do something. [*Crosses to settee—sits.*] I'll have the snow pushed off the roof, first thing in the morning.

MOLLY: No.

TONDER [*eagerly*]: Why not?

MOLLY: The people wouldn't trust me any more.

TONDER: I see. You *all* hate us. But I'd like to help you if you'll let me.

MOLLY [*rises. She is in control now. Her eyes narrow a little cruelly*]: Why do you ask? You are the conqueror. Your men don't *ask.* [*Crossing U.R.*] They *take* what they want.

TONDER [*rises, crosses to her*]: No. That's not what I want. That's not the way I want it.

MOLLY [*turns to him. Cruelly*]: You want me to like you, don't you, Lieutenant?

TONDER [*simply*]: Yes. You are so beautiful. So warm. [*She crosses to settee.*] I've seen no kindness in a woman's face for so long.

MOLLY [*turns to him*]: Do you see any in mine?

TONDER [*looking closely at her*]: I want to.

MOLLY [*she drops her eyes at last. Sits sofa*]: You are making love to me, aren't you, Lieutenant?

TONDER [*sits chair, front of stove. Clumsily*]: I want you to like me. Surely I want you to like me. I want to see it in your eyes. I've watched you in the street. I've even given orders you must not be molested. Have you been molested?

MOLLY [*quietly*]: No, I've not been molested.

TONDER: They told us the people would like us here. Would admire us. And they don't. They only hate us. [MOLLY *rises, crosses L. He changes the subject as though working against time.*] You are so beautiful.

MOLLY [*turns to him*]: You are beginning to make love to me, Lieutenant. You must go soon.

TONDER [*rises, crosses C.*]: A man needs love. A man dies without love. [MOLLY *crosses to chest.*] His insides shrivel, and his chest feels like a dry chip. I'm lonely.

MOLLY [*looking away from him*]: You'll want to go to bed with me, Lieutenant.

TONDER: I didn't say that. Why do you talk that way?

MOLLY [*turns to him, cruelly*]: Maybe I am trying to disgust you! I was married once. My husband is dead. [*Sits on chest. Her voice is bitter.*]

TONDER: I only want you to like me.

MOLLY: I know. You are a civilized man. You know that love-making is more full and whole and delightful if there is liking, too.

TONDER: Don't talk that way. [*Turns away, sits on settee.*]

MOLLY [*rises, crosses to him*]: We are a conquered people, Lieutenant. I am hungry. I will like you better if you feed me. My price is two sausages.

TONDER: You fooled me for a moment. But *you* hate me, too.

MOLLY [*crossing to chest*]: No. I don't hate you. I'm hungry. And—[*Turns to him.*] I hate you!

TONDER: I'll give you anything you need, but—

MOLLY [*interrupting*]: You want to call it something else? You don't want a whore. . . . Is that what you mean?

TONDER [*crosses to chair R., sits*]: I don't know what I mean! You make it sound full of hatred.

MOLLY: It's not nice to be hungry. Two sausages can be the most precious things in the world.

TONDER [*pleadingly*]: Don't say these things. Please don't.

MOLLY: Why not? [*Turns away to door.*] It's true.

TONDER [*rises, crosses C.*]: It is not true. This can't be true.

MOLLY: It isn't true. I don't hate you. I am lonely. [TONDER *sits on settee.* MOLLY *leans against door.*] The snow is heavy on the roof.

TONDER [*takes her hand. Places it to his cheek*]: Don't hate me. I'm only a soldier. I didn't ask to come here. You didn't ask to be my enemy. I am only a man, not a conquering man.

MOLLY [*stroking his head*]: I know.

TONDER: We have some little right to life.

MOLLY [*puts her cheek on his head*]: Yes. [*She leans a little toward him.*]

TONDER: I'll take care of you. We have some right to life in all the killing. [*She slowly straightens up. Suddenly she grows rigid, her eyes wide and staring as though she sees a vision. She draws away her hands sharply and crosses R.*] What is it? What's the matter. [*Her eyes stare straight ahead.*] What have I done?

MOLLY [*in a haunted voice—facing away from him*]: I dressed him in his best clothes like a little boy for his first day of school. I buttoned his shirt and tried to comfort him. But he was beyond comfort. [*Sits chair front of stove.*] And he was afraid.

TONDER [*rises*]: What are you saying?

MOLLY [*stares right ahead and seems to see what she is describing*]: I don't know why they let him come home. He didn't know what was happening. He didn't even kiss me when he went. He was afraid. And very brave. Like a little boy on his first day at school.

TONDER: That was your husband.

MOLLY: And then—he marched away—not very well nor steadily, and you took him out—and shot him. It was more strange than terrible then. I didn't quite believe it then.

TONDER: Your husband?

MOLLY: Yes, my husband. And now in the quiet house I believe it. Now with the heavy snow on the roof I believe it. And in the loneliness before day-break, in the half-warmed bed, I know it then.

TONDER [*he crosses to chest, picks up helmet, his face full of misery*]: Good night. [*Crosses to door, puts on helmet, turns to her.*] May I come back?

MOLLY [*staring at the memory*]: I don't know.

TONDER: Please let me come back.

MOLLY [*rises, crosses U.C. to table*]: No.

TONDER *looks at her for a moment and then goes quietly out the door.* MOLLY *crosses to settee, sits. Very silently* ANNIE *enters from kitchen R.*

ANNIE: There was a soldier here.

MOLLY: Yes, Annie.

ANNIE [*suspiciously*]: What was he doing here?

MOLLY [*her voice dreaming*]: He came to make love to me.

ANNIE [*crossing to her*]: Miss. What are you doing? You haven't joined them, have you? You aren't with them, like Corell?

MOLLY [*shaking her head*]: No. I'm not with them, Annie.

ANNIE: If he comes back while the Mayor's here it will be your fault.

MOLLY: He won't come back.

ANNIE [*very suspiciously*]: Shall I tell them to come in now? They're out behind the fence.

MOLLY: Yes. Tell them to come in.

ANNIE *exits L., leaving door open.* MOLLY *rises, crosses to chair R.* MOLLY *gets up. Shakes her head and tries to get alive again. There is a little sound in the passage and two tall blonde young men enter. They are dressed in pea-jackets and dark turtle-neck sweaters. They have stocking caps perched on their heads. They are wind-burned and strong and they look almost like twins. One is* WILL ANDERS, *and the other* TOM ANDERS.

WILL [*crossing R. takes off hat and gloves*]: Good evening, Molly. You heard?

TOM *enters, crosses to settee.*

MOLLY: Annie told me. It's a bad night to go.

TOM [*takes off hat*]: Better than a clear night. The planes see you on a clear night. What's the Mayor want, Molly?

MOLLY: I don't know. I heard about your brother. I'm sorry.

The two are silent. They look embarrassed.

TOM: Well, you know how it is, better than most.

MOLLY: Yes. I know.

Enter MAYOR. *He wears a fur-lined coat, hat, and gloves.*

MAYOR [*calls to* ANNIE]: Stand in the passage, Annie. Give us one knock for the patrol and one when it's gone. [*He closes door.*]

ANNIE [*off*]: Yes, sir.

MAYOR: Good evening, Molly.

MOLLY [*crossing to him to take his hat*]: Good evening Your Excellency. [*Takes hat to chest.*]

MAYOR: I got word you boys were going tonight.

MOLLY *comes to him for his gloves, takes them to chest.*

TOM: We have to go.

MAYOR [*nodding*]: Yes, I know.

TOM [*turns to* MAYOR]: You wanted to see us, sir?

MAYOR [*crossing to stove*]: Yes. I want to talk to you. I have a plan. Dr. Winter and I have discussed it.

A sharp knock on door. The room is silent. Every eye is turned toward the door. TOM *crosses to window.* WILL *steps toward door. Then first faintly, and growing louder, comes the tramp of the patrol. They near the door and their steps disappear in the distance. There is a second tap on the door. Those in the room relax.*

WILL: We haven't much time, sir.

MAYOR [*begins slowly*]: What I have to say won't take long. I want to speak simply. This is a little town. Justice and injustice are in terms of little things. The people are angry and they have no way to fight back. Our spirits and bodies aren't enough.

TOM: What can we do, sir?

MAYOR: We want to fight them and we can't. They are using hunger on the people now. Hunger brings weakness. You boys are sailing for England. Tell them to give us weapons.

Again there is a quick knock on the door and the people freeze where they are. The patrol comes by at double step. WILL *moves to the window.* TOM *goes into passage-way. The running steps come abreast of the house. There are muffled orders.*

SOLDIER: Break ranks!

SOLDIER: This way!

SOLDIER: Over here!

And the patrol runs on by. There is a second tap on the door.

MOLLY: They must be after someone.

Two rifle shots are heard in the distance.

WILL: I wonder if it's us?

TOM [*enters, uneasily to* WILL]: We should be going. [*To*
MAYOR.] Do you want guns, sir? Shall we ask for guns?

MAYOR: No. Tell them how it is. We are watched. Any
move we make calls for reprisal. If we could have simple
weapons, secret weapons. Weapons of stealth. Explosives.
Dynamite to blow out rails. Grenades if possible. Even
poison. [*He speaks angrily—crossing R.*] This is no honorable war. This is a war of treachery and murder. Let
us use the methods they have used on us. Let the British
bombers drop their great bombs on the works, but let
them also drop little bombs for us to use. To hide. To slip
under rails. Under trucks. Then we will be secretly armed,
and the invader will never know which of us is armed. Let
the bombers bring us simple weapons. We'll know how to
use them. [*Crosses D.R.*]

MOLLY *sits on settee.*

WILL: I've heard that in England there are still men in power
who do not dare to put weapons in the hands of common
people.

MAYOR: Oh. [*As though the wind had been knocked out of
him.*] I hadn't thought of that. Well, we can only see. If
such people still govern England and America, the world
is lost anyway. Tell them what we say if they will listen.
We must have help. But if we get it—[*His face grows
hard.*] we will help ourselves. Then the invader can never
rest again, never. We will blow up his supplies. [*Fiercely.*]
We will fight his rest and his sleep. We will fight his nerves
and his certainties.

TOM: If we get through, we'll tell them. Is that all, sir?

MAYOR: Yes, that's the core of it. [*Sits chair front stove.*]

TOM: What if they won't listen?

MAYOR: We can only try as you are trying the sea to-night.

The door opens and ANNIE *comes in quickly.*

ANNIE: There's a soldier coming up the path. [*She looks suspiciously at* MOLLY. MOLLY *rises. The others look at* MOLLY.] I locked the door.

There is a gentle knocking on outside door.

MAYOR [*rises in wonder*]: Molly, what is this? Are you in trouble?

MOLLY: No—No. Go out the back way. You can get out through the back. Hurry. [*She moves to entrance R.*]

TOM *and* WILL *hurry out R. through kitchen.* ANNIE *crosses to chest for* MAYOR'S *hat and gloves, takes them to him. He crosses to entrance, then turns to* MOLLY.

MAYOR: Do you want me to stay, Molly?

MOLLY: No. It will be all right.

MAYOR *exits.*

ANNIE [*cold with suspicion*]: It's the same soldier.

MOLLY [*crosses D.R.*]: Yes.

ANNIE: What's he want?

MOLLY [*crossing C.*]: I don't know.

ANNIE: Are you going to tell him anything?

MOLLY [*wonderingly*]: No. [*Then sharply turning to her.*] No!

ANNIE [*quietly*]: Good night, then. [*Crosses to entrance R.*]

MOLLY [*crossing to front settee*]: Good night, Annie. Don't worry about me. [*Crosses to* ANNIE.]

ANNIE: Good night. [*Exits.*]

MOLLY *stands watching her off. The knocking comes again. She crosses to settee. The knocking is repeated. She turns sharply and sits on settee. Her hand falls on the scissors she left on the settee earlier. She picks them up and looks at them intently. Again the knocking comes.*

She rises and places the scissors in her hand, dagger fashion. Then turns to lamp on table, turns it low and the room becomes nearly dark. The knocking is repeated. She crosses to door, throws it open.

MOLLY [*her voice is stricken*]: I'm coming, Lieutenant—I'm coming.

CURTAIN

PART TWO: SCENE III

TIME: *Three weeks later. It is morning.*

SCENE: *Living-room of the Palace of the* MAYOR. *The dining-table remains as it was placed the day* MORDEN *was shot. The room has become austere. It has lost the grace it had. And the comfort. Chairs are about the table, leaving the walls looking blank, and on the table a few papers are scattered, making it look like a business office.*

The armchair used at the beginning of the play is now in front of the stove. A card table is against wall L. in place of the cot bed. 3 chairs are around it. Empty beer bottles, tin cups, cigarette butts, and playing cards are on the table. The table C. has a chair at each end and one in the center above table. The blackout curtains are open. Otherwise the room is as we last saw it.

It is a dark day, overcast with clouds.

AT RISE: *As the curtain goes up,* ANNIE *comes out of the* MAYOR'S *room left. And on the way to the other entrance she swoops by the table looking at the papers that lie there. The door U.L. opens.* LOFT *comes in. He sees* ANNIE.

LOFT [*crossing to table*]: What are you doing here?

ANNIE [*sullenly*]: Yes, sir. [*Crosses to R. end table.*]

LOFT [*crossing to above table*]: I said, what are you doing here?

SOLDIER *enters U.L., stands at door awaiting orders.*

ANNIE: I thought to clean up, sir.

LOFT: Let things alone and go along.

ANNIE: Yes, sir. [*She exits quickly out of door R.*]

LOFT *takes off helmet. A* SOLDIER *standing at door holds a number of blue packages, to the ends of which dangle strings and little pieces of cloth.*

LOFT: Put them on the table. [*The* SOLDIER *gingerly lays packages on table.*] That's all.

The SOLDIER *wheels and leaves the room.* LOFT *goes to front of table and picks up one of the packages. His face wears a look of distaste. He holds up the little cloth attached to the package. Holds it above his head and drops it. The cloth opens to a tiny parachute. And the package floats to the floor.* LOFT *picks up package and examines it.*

LANSER [*coming quickly into the room, carrying a blue paper, followed by* HUNTER, *who has a square of yellow paper in his hand.* LANSER, *in a business-like tone*]: Good morning, Captain. [*He goes to chair C. above table and sits down. For a moment he looks at the little pile of packages, then picks one up and holds it. Speaks curtly.*] Have you examined these?

HUNTER [*pulls out chair L. end table and sits down. He looks at the yellow paper in his hand*]: Not very carefully. There are three breaks in the railroad, all within ten miles.

LOFT *crosses to R. end table, takes off coat, puts it on chair.*

LANSER: Well, take a look at them and see what you think of them.

HUNTER [*reaches for a package, strips off outer blue cover. Inside there are two items, a tube and a square package.* HUNTER *takes out his knife and cuts into tube.* LOFT *looks over his shoulder.* HUNTER *smells the cut place. Feels the material and rubs it between his two fingers*]: It's silly. It's commercial dynamite. I don't know what percent nitroglycerine until I test it. [*He looks at end of tube. It has an ordinary dynamite cap, fulminate mercury, and about a one-minute fuse. He tosses the tube on table.*] Very cheap. Very simple.

LANSER [*looking at* LOFT]: How many do you think were dropped?

LOFT: I don't know, sir. We picked up about fifty. But we found ninety more parachutes with nothing on them. The people must have hidden those packages.

LANSER: It doesn't really matter. They can drop as many as they want. We can't stop it. And we can't use it back against them. They haven't conquered anybody.

LOFT [*crosses to chair R. end table*]: We can beat them off the face of the earth. [*Sits.*]

HUNTER *is prying copper cap out of the top of one of the sticks.*

LANSER: Yes, we can do that. Have you looked at this wrapper, Hunter?

HUNTER: Not yet. I haven't had time.

LANSER [*quietly*]: Well, I have. It's kind of devilish, this thing. The wrapper is blue so it is easy to see. Take off the outer paper and here—[*He picks up smaller package and unwraps it.*]—Here is a piece of chocolate. Everybody will be looking for these things. Even our own soldiers will steal the chocolate. Children'll be looking for them like Easter eggs. [*A* SOLDIER *comes in U.L. and lays a square of yellow paper in front of* LANSER.] That's all. [SOLDIER *exits U.L.* LANSER *glances at it and laughs harshly.*] Here is something for you, Hunter. Two more breaks in your line.

LOFT: Did they drop them everywhere?

LANSER: Now that's the funny thing. I've talked to the Capitol. This is the only place they dropped them.

HUNTER: What do you make of that?

LANSER: Well, it's hard to say. I think this might be a test. If it works here they'll use it all over. And if it doesn't work here, they won't bother.

LOFT: Well, what are we going to do?

LANSER: I have orders to stamp this out so ruthlessly that it will stop right here.

HUNTER: How am I going to mend five breaks in a railroad? I haven't rails enough.

LANSER: Rip out some old siding.

HUNTER: That'll make a hell of a road-bed. [HUNTER *tosses the tube he has torn apart on the pile.*]

LOFT: We must stop this thing at once, sir. We must arrest and punish the people who pick these things up. We must get busy so that they won't think we are weak.

LANSER [*smiling at him*]: Take it easy. Let's see what we have first and then we'll think of remedies. [*He takes a new package from pile and unwraps it. He unwraps the chocolate and tastes it.*] This is a devilish thing. Good chocolate, too. I can't even resist it myself. The prize in the grab-bag. [*He picks up the dynamite.*] How effective is this, Hunter?

HUNTER: Very effective for small jobs. Dynamite with a cap and a one-minute fuse. Good if you know how to use it. No good if you don't.

LANSER [*he is studying the print on inside of wrapper*]: Listen to this. They'll know how to use it—[*Reading from paper.*] "To the Unconquered People. Hide this. Do not expose yourself. Do not try to do large things with it."

[*He begins to skip through.*] Now here: "Rails in the country—work at night—tie up transportation." Now here—instructions: "Rails. Place stick under rail, close to joint and tight against tie. Pack mud or hard-packed snow around it so that it is firm. When fuse is lighted, you have a slow count of sixty before it explodes." [LANSER *looks up at* HUNTER.]

HUNTER: It works.

LANSER [*looks back at his paper and skips through*]: "Bridges: Weaken but do not destroy." And here— "Transmission poles." And here: "Culverts—trucks." [*He lays paper down.*] Well, there it is.

LOFT [*angrily*]: We must do something. There must be a way to control this. What does Headquarters say?

LANSER [*purses his lips and his fingers play with one of the tubes*]: I could have told you what they would say before they said it. I have the order. "Set booby traps. Poison the chocolate." [*He pauses for a moment. Rises, crosses R. to stove.*] Hunter, I am a good loyal man, but sometimes when I hear the brilliant ideas of Headquarters, I wish I were a civilian. An old crippled civilian. The leaders always think they're dealing with stupid people. I don't say that this is the measure of their intelligence—do I?

HUNTER [*looking amused*]: Do you?

LOFT *looks up at* LANSER.

LANSER [*sharply*]: No. I don't. [*Crossing to front of table.*] But what will happen? One man will pick one of these and get blown to bits by our booby trap. One kid will eat chocolate and die of strychnine poisoning. And then—[*He looks down at his hands.*]—they'll poke them with poles or lasso them before they touch them. They'll try the chocolate on the cat. God damn it! [*Sits against table.*] These are intelligent people. Stupid traps won't catch them twice.

HUNTER: Why do you suppose it was only dropped here?

LANSER: For one of two reasons. [*Crossing to card table.*] Either this town was picked at random. Or else there is communication between this town and the outside. We know that some of the young men have got away.

LOFT [*rises. Repeating*]: We must do something. [*Slaps table.*]

LANSER [*angrily. He picks up some of the cards and shuffles them*]: Loft, I think I'll recommend you for the General Staff. You want to get to work before you even know what the problem is. This is a new kind of conquest. Always before it was possible to disarm people and keep them in ignorance. Now they listen to their radios and we can't stop them. [*He sits astraddle chair R. of table facing* LOFT.] They read handbills. Weapons drop from the sky for them. Now it's dynamite. Soon grenades. Then poison.

LOFT [*anxiously, rises, crosses C. front of table*]: They haven't dropped poison.

LANSER [*folding a card into a dart*]: No, but they will. Can you think what would happen to the morale of our men, or even to you, if the people had some of those little game darts? The points coated with cyanide. Silent deadly things. [*Throws card dart at* LOFT, *who steps back.*] What if you knew arsenic was about? Would you eat or drink comfortably?

HUNTER [*dryly*]: Are you writing the enemy's campaign?

LANSER: I am trying to anticipate it.

LOFT: We sit here talking. [*Crossing R.C.*] We should be looking for this dynamite. If there's organization among these people we have to find it, [*Crosses to R. end above table.*] and stamp it out.

LANSER: Yes. [*Rises, throws cards on table.*] We have to stamp it out, ferociously. [*Crosses R. to armchair.*] You take a detail, Loft. Get Prackle to take one. I wish we had more Junior officers. I wish we hadn't lost Tonder. [*Sits armchair.*]

LOFT: I don't like the way Lieutenant Prackle is acting, sir.

LANSER: What's he doing?

LOFT [*putting on his coat*]: Well, he's nervous and irritable. He's not himself at all.

LANSER: Yes, I know. That's the thing I talked about so much. [*He chuckles.*] I might have been a Major-General if I hadn't talked about it so much. We trained our young men for victory. They are glorious in victory. They don't know how to act in defeat. We told them they were brighter and braver than other young men. It's a shock to them to find that they aren't a bit brighter or braver than other young men.

LOFT [*crosses to* LANSER. *Harshly*]: What do you mean, defeat? We aren't defeated. [LANSER *looks coldly at him for a long moment. He doesn't speak, and finally* LOFT'S *eyes waver.*] Sir!

LANSER: Thank you.

LOFT: You don't demand it of the others, sir.

LANSER: They don't think about it, so it isn't an insult. When you leave it out it is insulting.

LOFT: Yes, sir.

LANSER: Go now. Start your search. [LOFT *crosses to table, picks up helmet. Crosses L.C.* LANSER *rises.*] I don't want any shooting unless there's an overt act. You understand?

LOFT: Yes, sir. [*Salutes formally and goes out of the room U.L.*]

LANSER *crosses U.R. to windows.*

HUNTER: You were a little rough on him.

LANSER: Had to be. [*Crosses to table—picks up piece of*

dynamite.] He's frightened. I know his kind. He has to be disciplined when he is afraid or he will go to pieces. He relies on discipline the way other men rely on sympathy. I suppose you'd better get to your rails. Tonight's the time when they'll really blow them. [*Sits chair above table.*]

HUNTER: Yes. [*Rises, crosses to door U.L.*] I suppose the orders are coming from the Capitol?

LANSER: Yes.

HUNTER [*crossing back to him*]: Are they—?

LANSER: You know what they are. Take the leaders. Shoot the leaders. Take hostages. Shoot the hostages. Take more hostages. Shoot them. [*His voice has risen and now it sinks almost to a whisper.*] And the hatred growing. And the hurt between us deeper and deeper.

HUNTER [*quietly*]: Colonel, do you want me to recommend— maybe you are overtired, Colonel? Could I say you are overtired?

LANSER [*covers his eyes with his hands for a moment. Then his shoulders straighten and his face grows hard*]: I'm not a civilian, Hunter. We are short enough of officers already. You know that. Get to your work, Major.

HUNTER [*clicks heels*]: Sir. [*He goes out the door and says.*] Yes. He's in there.

PRACKLE [*comes in, carrying helmet, crosses to chair L. of table. His face sullen and belligerent*]: Colonel Lanser, sir. I wish to—

LANSER: Sit down. Sit down. [PRACKLE *sits chair L. of table, puts helmet on table.*] Rest a moment. Be a good soldier, Lieutenant.

PRACKLE [*the stiffness goes out of him. He sits down heavily*]: I wish—

LANSER: Don't talk for a moment. I know what it is. You didn't think it would be this way.

PRACKLE [*rises, crosses to R. end table*]: They hate us. They hate us so.

LANSER [*smiling wryly*]: I wonder if I know what it is. [PRACKLE *turns to him.*] It takes young men to make good soldiers. Young men need young women, is that it? [*Kindly.*] Does she hate you?

PRACKLE [*looks at him in amazement*]: I don't know, sir. [*Turns away.*] Sometimes she's only sorry.

LANSER: And you're pretty miserable.

PRACKLE [*crosses to chair R. of table, sits*]: I don't like it here, sir.

LANSER: No. You thought it would be fun. Lieutenant Tonder went to pieces. And then he went out and got himself killed. I could send you home. Do you want to be sent home, knowing we need you here?

PRACKLE [*uneasily*]: No, sir.

LANSER [*rises, crosses around to front of table, leans against table*]: Good. Now I'll tell you. And I hope you'll understand. You're not a man any more. You're a soldier. Your comfort is of no importance and your life not very much. If you live you will have memories. That's about all you will have. You must take orders and carry them out. Most of them will be unpleasant. But that's not your business. I will not lie to you, Lieutenant. They should have trained you for this. Not for cheers and flowers. [*His voice hardens; he gets to his feet.*] But you took the job. Will you stay with it, or quit it? We cannot take care of your soul.

PRACKLE [*stands up*]: Thank you, sir.

SOLDIER [*enters U.L.*]: Mr. Corell to see you, sir.

LANSER: Send him in. [SOLDIER *exits.* LANSER *crosses around to above table.*] And the girl, Lieutenant. You may rape her or protect her or marry her. That is of no importance, as long as you shoot her when it is ordered. You may go now.

PRACKLE *crosses L., picks up helmet, exits.* LANSER *sits*

and busies himself with his work. CORELL *enters. But he is a changed man. And his expression is no longer jovial nor friendly. His face is sharp and bitter; he carries his hat and coat, puts them on chair L. of table.*

CORELL: I should have come before, Colonel, but your lack of cooperation made me hesitant.

LANSER: Cooperation? You were waiting for a reply to your private report to the Capitol, I remember.

CORELL [*crossing around to above table L. of* LANSER]: I was waiting for much more than that. You refused me a position of authority. You said I was valueless. You did not realize that I was in this town long before you were. You left the Mayor in his office, contrary to my advice.

LANSER: Without him there might have been more disorder than there has been.

CORELL: That's a matter of opinion. This man is the leader of a rebellious people.

LANSER: He's just a simple man.

CORELL: You forget, Colonel, that I had my sources. Mayor Orden has been in constant contact with every happening in this community. On the night when Lieutenant Tonder was murdered, he was in the house where the murder was committed. When the girl escaped to the hills she stayed with one of his relatives. I traced her there but she was gone. When men have escaped, Orden has known about it and helped. I strongly suspect that he is in back of these little parachutes.

LANSER [*eagerly*]: But you can't prove it.

CORELL: The first things I know. The last I can't prove yet. Perhaps now you'll be willing to listen to me.

LANSER [*quietly*]: What do you suggest?

CORELL: These suggestions are a little stronger than suggestions, Colonel. Orden must now be a hostage. And

his life must depend on the peacefulness of this community. His life must depend on the lighting of one single
fuse. [*Reaches into pocket and brings out a little folding
book such as is used for identification. He flips it open
and lays it in front of* LANSER.] This was the answer to
my report, sir.

LANSER [*looks at book and speaks quietly*]: Um—you
really did go over my head, didn't you? [*He looks up at*
CORELL *with frank dislike in his eyes.*]

CORELL: Now, Colonel, must I suggest more strongly than
I have that Mayor Orden must be held hostage?

LANSER: He's here. He hasn't escaped. [*Rises, crosses to R.
end table.*] How can we hold him more hostage than we
are?

*In the distance there is an explosion, and both men look
around in the direction from which it comes.*

CORELL [*a step to him*]: There it is. If this experiment
succeeds, there will be dynamite in every conquered
country.

LANSER [*quietly*]: What do you suggest?

CORELL: Orden must be held against rebellion.

LANSER: And if rebellion comes and we shoot Orden?

CORELL: Then that doctor's next. He's the next in
authority.

LANSER: He holds no office. Well, suppose we shoot him—
What then?

CORELL: Then rebellion is broken before it starts.

LANSER [*shakes his head a little sadly*]: Have you ever
thought that one execution makes a hundred active enemies where we have passive enemies? Even patriotism
is not as sharp as personal hurt, personal loss. A dead
brother, a dead father—that really arms an enemy.

CORELL [*almost as though he had grounds for blackmail*

now]: Your attitude, sir, may lead you to trouble. It is fortunate that I am—your friend.

LANSER [*crosses R. to arm chair; with a little contempt in his voice*]· I can see your report almost as though it were in front of me—

CORELL [*quickly*]: Oh! But you're mistaken, sir. I haven't—

LANSER [*turns to him*]: This war should be for the very young. They would have the proper spirit, but unfortunately they are not able to move guns and men about. I suffer from civilization. That means I can know one thing and do another. I know we have failed—I knew we would before we started. The thing the leader wanted to do cannot be done.

CORELL [*excitedly, leaning toward him across table*]: What is this? What do you say?

LANSER [*quietly, crosses to R. end of table*]: Oh! Don't worry. I will go about it as though it could be done and do a better job than the zealots could. And when the tide turns, I may save a few lives, from knowing how to retreat.

CORELL: They shouldn't have sent a man like you here!

LANSER: Don't worry—as long as we can hold, we will hold. [*Crossing to* CORELL, *sadly.*] I can act quite apart from my knowledge. I will shoot the Mayor. [*His voice grows hard.*] I will not break the rules. I will shoot the doctor, I will help tear and burn the world. I don't like you, Corell. I am licking my wounds surely. And—I am giving you wounds to lick. [*Crosses around to front of table R. end.*] Sergeant!

SERGEANT [*enters U.L., crosses D.L.C.*]: Sir?

LANSER [*slowly*]: Place Mayor Orden and Dr. Winter under arrest!

SERGEANT *turns, exits.* LANSER *crosses to doors U.L.*

and exits. CORELL *looks after them, then turns back to table, looks at it, places his hands on it, then slowly seats himself in the chair* LANSER *vacated.*

CURTAIN

PART TWO: SCENE IV

TIME: *About half an hour later.*
  SCENE: *The same as before.*
  AT RISE: *The table has been cleaned up. One* SOLDIER *stands to the R. of doors U.L.* MAYOR *is standing at the R. window looking out.*

MAYOR [*crossing to table*]: Where is Colonel Lanser? [*The* SOLDIER *does not answer.*] Please tell Colonel Lanser I wish to see him. [MAYOR *turns and crosses R. As he does* WINTER *enters U.L. followed by a* SOLDIER. MAYOR *turns to them.*] Doctor.

WINTER [*crossing to chair L. end table*]: Well, Your Excellency. This is one time you didn't send for me. I guess we're being held as hostages.

MAYOR [*crossing to him*]: Well, we've been together in everything else. I suppose it was bound to come. They're afraid of us now. I'm glad it's come.

WINTER: They think that because they have only one leader and one head that we are like that. They know that ten heads lopped off would destroy them. [*Crosses to chair L. of table, sits.*] But we are a free people. We have as many heads as we have people. Leaders pop up like mushrooms in a time of need.

MAYOR [*crossing L. to chair, patting* WINTER'S *shoulder as he passes above him*]: Thank you. I knew it, but it is good to hear you say it. The people won't go under, will they?

WINTER: No. They'll grow stronger with outside help.

MAYOR [sits chair L.C.]: I can talk to you, Doctor. I'm thinking of my own death. If they follow the usual course, they must kill me, and then they must kill you. [WINTER is silent.] Mustn't they?

WINTER: I guess so.

MAYOR: You know so. [He is silent a moment.] I am a little man in a little town. But there must be a spark in little men that can burst into flame. At first I was afraid. I thought of all the things I might do to save my own life. And then that went away and now I feel a kind of exaltation, as though I were bigger and better than I am. It's like—well, do you remember in school, a long time ago, I delivered Socrates' denunciation? I was exalted then, too.

WINTER: You were indeed.

MAYOR: I was Socrates. I denounced the school board. I bellowed at them. And I could see their faces grow red.

WINTER: They were holding their breaths to keep from laughing. I remember well. It was graduation and your shirt tail was sticking out.

MAYOR [raises his head, looks at the ceiling]: Um—Um—Um—How did it go?

WINTER: Let me see—it begins—[Prompting him.] "And now, Oh men."

MAYOR [softly]: "And now, oh men who have condemned me—

I would fain prophesy to you—

For I am about to die—"

LANSER comes quietly into the room, crosses above table to R. end and stops on hearing the word. MAYOR looks at the ceiling, lost in trying to remember.

"And—in the hour of death—

Men are gifted with prophetic power.
And I—prophesy to you, who are my murderers,
That immediately after my—
my death—"

WINTER [*breaking in*]: Departure.

MAYOR: What?

WINTER: The word is departure, not death. You made the
same mistake before.

MAYOR: No. It's death. [LANSER *puts his helmet on table.*
MAYOR *looks around and sees* LANSER *watching him.*]
Isn't it death?

LANSER: "Departure. Immediately after my departure."

WINTER: You see. That's two against one. Departure is the
word.

MAYOR [*looking straight ahead. His eyes in memory. Seeing
nothing outward*]:
"I prophesy to you who are my murderers,
That immediately after my departure,
Punishment far heavier than you have inflicted upon me
Will surely await you.
Me you have killed because you wanted to escape the
accuser
And not to give an account of your lives . . ."
[*Softly.*] "But that will not be as you suppose—far
otherwise."
[*His voice grows stronger.*] "For I say that there will be more
accusers of you than there are now,
Accusers whom hitherto I have restrained.
If you think that by killing men, you can prevent someone
from censoring your lives—you are mistaken."
[*He thinks for a time, smiles embarrassedly.*] That's all I can
remember.

WINTER: It's very good after forty-six years.

LANSER: Mayor Orden, I have arrested you as a hostage.
For the good behavior of your people. These are my orders.

MAYOR [*simply*]: You don't understand. When I become a hindrance to the people, they'll do without me.

LANSER [*crossing R. to armchair*]: The people know you will be shot if they light another fuse. [*Turns to him.*] Will they light it?

MAYOR: They will light the fuse.

LANSER: Suppose you ask them not to?

MAYOR [*looks at him, slowly*]: I am not a very brave man, sir. I think they will light it anyway. I hope they will. But if I ask them not to, they will be sorry.

LANSER: But they will light it?

MAYOR: Yes, they will light it. I have no choice of living or dying, you see, sir. But—I do have a choice of how I do it. If I tell them not to fight, they will be sorry. But they will fight. If I tell them to fight, they will be glad. And I, who am not a very brave man, will have made them a little braver. [*He smiles apologetically.*] It's an easy thing to do, since the end for me is the same.

LANSER [*crossing to armchair R.*]: If you say yes, we will tell them you said no. [WINTER *rises.*] We will tell them you begged for your life. [*Sits.*]

WINTER [*angrily, crossing to* LANSER]: They would know. You don't keep secrets. One of your men got out of hand one night and he said the flies had conquered the fly-paper. Now the whole nation knows his words. They have made a song of it. You do not keep secrets. [*Crosses U.R. to table.*]

LANSER: Mayor Orden, I think a proclamation from you might save many lives.

MAYOR [*quietly*]: Nothing can change it. You will be destroyed and driven out.

MADAME [*enters U.L., crosses to* MAYOR]: What is this all about?

LANSER *rises.*

MAYOR: Be quiet a moment, dear. [*His voice is very soft.*] The people don't like to be conquered, sir. And so they will not be. Free men cannot start a war. But once it is started, they can fight on in defeat. Herd men, followers of a leader, they cannot do that. And so it is always that herd men win battles, but free men win wars. You will find it is so, sir.

LANSER [*crosses to R. end table*]: My orders are clear. [*Looks at watch.*] Eleven o'clock is the dead-line. I have taken my hostages. If there is violence I will execute them.

WINTER [*crosses D. to R. of* LANSER]: And you will carry out the orders, knowing they will fail.

From the distance there is the sound of an explosion. LANSER *looks at* WINTER. *They stand tensely listening and a second explosion comes.* LANSER *and* MAYOR *look toward windows.*

LANSER: I will carry out my orders.

MADAME: I wish you would tell me what all this nonsense is.

LANSER *picks up his helmet from table.*

MAYOR [*turns to her, takes her hand*]: It's nonsense, dear.

MADAME: But they can't arrest the Mayor.

MAYOR: No, they can't arrest the Mayor. The Mayor is an idea conceived by free men. [*To* LANSER.] It will escape arrest.

MADAME: You've forgotten it again. You always forget— Wait here. I'll get it for you. [*Exits U.L.*]

LANSER [*crosses to L.C., puts on helmet, clicks heels, bows*]: Your Excellency! [*Exits U.L.—front door is heard to slam.*]

MAYOR *turns to* WINTER, *they exchange glances,* WINTER *crosses to stove.*

MAYOR [*calls*]: Annie. [*The door R. opens instantly.*] Listening?

ANNIE: Yes, sir. [*Crosses to him.*]

MAYOR [*smiles, takes her hands*]: Annie, stay with Madame as long as she needs you. Don't leave her alone. [*Kisses her on forehead.*]

ANNIE: I'll take care of her, Your Excellency. [*Turns away, exits R.*]

MAYOR: Doctor, how did it go about the flies?

DOCTOR: The flies have conquered the fly-paper.

MAYOR [*chuckling to himself*]: The flies have conquered the fly-paper.

MADAME [*enters U.L., carrying* MAYOR'S *chain of office, crosses to him*]: You always forget it. [*Places chain around his neck.*]

MAYOR [*looks at her. Puts his arm about her shoulders. Uses the same tone as earlier. He knows what she is doing*]: My dear—my very dear. [*Kisses her on cheek.*]

MADAME: Annie and Joseph are up to something in the kitchen. [*She crosses to R.C.*] I'll just have to . . . [*She stops as though to recall something, then crosses back to* MAYOR, *kisses him on the mouth, straightens his hair, and starts again for the kitchen.*] I'll just have to see what they're up to. [*Exits R.*]

PRACKLE *enters from U.L., comes to attention above table. The two* SOLDIERS *snap to attention and shoulder their bayoneted rifles.*

MAYOR [*turns to look at the* SOLDIERS, *then takes out his watch, turns to* WINTER]: Eleven o'clock.

WINTER: A time-minded people. [*He crosses to* MAYOR *who takes his watch and chain and puts them in* WINTER'S *hand, then clasps his hands. They look at each other a moment, then* MAYOR *turns and crosses L.C. There he stops and turns back to* WINTER.] "Crito, I owe a cock to Ascalaepius. Will you remember to pay the debt?"

WINTER [*crosses C. to table*]: "The debt shall be paid."

MAYOR [*chuckling*]: I remembered that one.

WINTER [*very softly*]: Yes. You remembered it.

MAYOR: The debt will be paid! [*He turns and walks slowly to the door as another explosion is heard, this time closer.*]

PRACKLE *goes ahead of him. The* SOLDIERS *follow him out as the*

CURTAIN
COMES DOWN SLOWLY

PROPERTIES

Ash tray
Watch for Dr. Winter
Watch for Mayor
Mantle ornament
Pipe
Submachine gun
Small card
Heavy gold chain
Double-barrelled shotgun
Sporting rifle
Silver cigarette box with cigarettes and safety matches
Several cups of coffee
Maps, microscope, rock and ore specimens
Various paper documents
Drawing board, triangle, paper drawing, pen, pencils,
    etc., and velvet-lined box for pen
Shaving brush
Field glasses
Side arm and other small military equipment for wearing
Gas mask bag
Brown canvas, tube, iron tripod base, metal rod
Folded rotogravure page with pictures of undraped girls
Nail
White bandage for Correll
Several newspapers
Small dagger (side arm for Lanser)

The Acts of King Arthur and His Noble Knights
Edited by Chase Horton with a Foreword by Christopher Paolini
In his only work of fantasy literature, John Steinbeck retells Malory's beloved Arthurian stories. *ISBN 978-0-14-310545-9*

America and Americans and Selected Nonfiction
Edited by Susan Shillinglaw and Jackson J. Benson
This comprehensive volume brings together more than fifty of Steinbeck's finest essays and journalistic pieces. *ISBN 978-0-14-243741-4*

Bombs Away
Introduction by James H. Meredith
On the heels of the enormous success of his masterwork *The Grapes of Wrath*, John Steinbeck, wrote *Bombs Away*, a nonfiction account of his experiences with U.S. Army Air Force bomber crews during World War II. *ISBN 978-0-14-310591-6*

Burning Bright
Introduction by John Ditsky
This novel traces the story of a man ignorant of his own sterility, a wife who commits adultery to give her husband a child, the father of that child, and the outsider whose actions affect them all. *ISBN 978-0-14-303944-0*

Cannery Row
Introduction and Notes by Susan Shillinglaw
Steinbeck's tough but loving portrait evokes the lives of Monterey's vital laboring class and their emotional triumph over the bleak existence of life in Cannery Row.
ISBN 978-0-14-018737-3

Cup of Gold
Introduction by Susan F. Beegel
Steinbeck's first novel, and the only historical novel he ever wrote, brings to life the exciting, violent adventures of the infamous pirate Henry Morgan.
ISBN 978-0-14-303945-7

East of Eden
Introduction by David Wyatt
The masterpiece of Steinbeck's later years, this is the powerful and vastly ambitious novel that is both family saga and a modern retelling of the book of Genesis.
ISBN 978-0-14-018639-0

The Grapes of Wrath
Introduction and Notes by Robert DeMott
This Pulitzer Prize-winning epic of the Great Depression follows the western movement of one family and a nation in search of work and human dignity.

"I think, and with earnest and honest consideration . . . that *The Grapes of Wrath* is the greatest American novel I have ever read." —Dorothy Parker
ISBN 978-0-14-303943-3

In Dubious Battle
Introduction and Notes by Warren French
This powerful social novel, set in the California apple country, is a story of labor unrest in the migrant community and the search for identity of its protagonist, young Jim Nolan. *ISBN 978-0-14-303963-1*

The Log from the Sea of Cortez
Introduction by Richard Astro
This exciting day-by-day account of Steinbeck's trip to the Gulf of California with biologist Ed Ricketts is a wonderful combination of science, philosophy, and adventure. *ISBN 978-0-14-018744-1*

The Long Valley
Introduction by John H. Timmerman
This collection of stories set in Salinas Valley includes the O. Henry Prize-winning story "The Murder." *ISBN 978-0-14-018745-8*

The Moon is Down
Introduction by Donald V. Coers
In this masterful tale set in Norway during World War II, Steinbeck explores the effects of invasion on both the conquered and the conquerors.
ISBN 978-0-14-018746-5

Of Mice and Men
Introduction by Susan Shillinglaw
A parable about commitment, loneliness, hope, and loss, *Of Mice and Men* remains one of America's most widely read and beloved novels. *ISBN 978-0-14-018642-0*

Once There Was a War
Edited by Mark Bowden
Steinbeck's dispatches filed from the front lines during World War II vividly evoke the human side of the war. *ISBN 978-0-14-310479-7*

The Pastures of Heaven
Introduction and Notes by James Nagel
Each of these tales is devoted to a family living in a fertile valley on the outskirts of Monterey, California, and the effects that one family has on all of them.
ISBN 978-0-14-018748-9

The Pearl
Introduction by Linda Wagner-Martin with Drawings by José Clemente Orozco
The diver Kino believes that his discovery of a beautiful pearl means the promise of a better life for his impoverished family. *ISBN 978-0-14-018738-0*

The Portable John Steinbeck
Edited by Pascal Covici, Jr.
This collection includes *Of Mice and Men* and *The Red Pony*, as well as excerpts from many of his other books, short stories, and his 1962 Nobel Prize Acceptance Speech. *ISBN 978-0-14-015002-5*

The Red Pony
Introduction by John Seelye
When young Jody forges a special connection with a hot-tempered pony named Gabilian, he discovers that he still has much to learn about the ways of nature and, also, the ways of man. *ISBN 978-0-14-018739-7*

A Russian Journal
With Photographs by Robert Capa
Introduction by Susan Shillinglaw
A remarkable memoir and unique historical document that records the writer and acclaimed war photographer's journey through Cold War Russia.

ISBN 978-0-14-118019-9

The Short Novels of John Steinbeck
Collected here for the first time in a deluxe paperback volume are six of John Steinbeck's most widely read and beloved novels—*Tortilla Flat, The Red Pony, Of Mice and Men, The Moon Is Down, Cannery Row,* and *The Pearl.*

ISBN 978-0-14-310577-0

The Short Reign of Pippin IV
Edited with an Introduction by Robert E. Morsberger and Katherine Morsberger
Steinbeck's only work of political satire turns the French Revolution upside down, creating the hilarious characters of the motley royal court of King Pippin.

ISBN 978-0-14-303946-4

To a God Unknown
Introduction and Notes by Robert DeMott
Set in familiar Steinbeck territory, this mystical tale explores one man's attempt to control the forces of nature and, ultimately, to understand the ways of God.

ISBN 978-0-14-018751-9

Tortilla Flat
Introduction by Thomas Fensch
Adopting the structure and themes of the Arthurian legend, Steinbeck created a "Camelot" on a hillside on the California coast and peopled it with a colorful band of knights, spinning a tale as compelling as the famous legends of the Round Table.

ISBN 978-0-14-018740-3

Travels with Charley in Search of America
Introduction by Jay Parini
This chronicle of Steinbeck and his poodle Charley's 1960 trip across America meanders from small towns to growing cities to glorious wilderness oases.

ISBN 978-0-14-018741-0

The Wayward Bus
Introduction by Gary Scharnhorst
In this imaginative and unsentimental chronicle of a bus traveling California's back roads, Steinbeck creates a vivid assortment of characters, all running away from their shattered dreams but hoping that they are running toward the promise of a future.

ISBN 978-0-14-243787-2

The Winter of Our Discontent
Introduction and Notes by Susan Schillinglaw
Ethan Hawley works as a clerk in the grocery store owned by an Italian immigrant. His wife is restless, and his teenaged children are hungry for the tantalizing material comforts he cannot provide. Then one day, in a moment of moral crisis, Ethan decides to take a holiday from his own scrupulous standards.

ISBN 978-0-14-018753-3